SECOND EDITION

Brain–
Compatible
Assessments

SECOND EDITION

Brain-
Compatible
Assessments

Diane
Ronis

Foreword by
Renate
Nummela
Caine

CORWIN PRESS
A SAGE Publications Company
Thousand Oaks, CA 91320

For information:

Corwin Press
A Sage Publications Company
2455 Teller Road
Thousand Oaks, California 91320
www.corwinpress.com

Sage Publications Ltd
1 Oliver's Yard
55 City Road
London EC1Y 1SP
United Kingdom

Sage Publications India Pvt. Ltd.
B-42, Panchsheel Enclave
Post Box 4109
New Delhi 110 017 India

Printed in the United States of America on acid-free paper

Library of Congress Cataloging-in-Publication Data

Ronis, Diane L.
Brain-compatible assessments / Diane Ronis.—2nd ed.
     p. cm.
Includes bibliographical references and index.
ISBN-13: 978-1-4129-5020-6 (cloth)
ISBN-13: 978-1-4129-5021-3 (pbk.)
  1. Educational tests and measurements. 2. Learning, Psychology of. I. Title.

LB3051.R597 2007
371.26'4—dc22

2006034105

06   07   08   09   10   10   9   8   7   6   5   4   3   2   1

Acquisitions Editor:	Jean Ward
Editorial Assistant:	Jordan Barbakow
Production Editor:	Sanford Robinson
Copy Editor:	Colleen Brennan
Typesetter:	C&M Digitals (P) Ltd.
Cover Designer:	Rose Storey
Graphic Designer:	Karine Hovsepian
Indexer:	Julie Grayson

Contents

Foreword

To say that these are conflicting times in education, and specifically for educational assessment, is to greatly understate the degree of turbulence both inside and outside the classroom. Certainly the very least that everyone agrees on is that students need to know how to read well, write well, and do mathematics. Beyond those basics, the necessary skills required by tomorrow's workforce are very different from what most schools are still doing. Corporate trainers assure us that learning benchmarked only by paper and pencil tests will be sufficient only for those working at the lowest level of the workforce. As a participant at a Schools for the 21st Century Conference told us,

> Imagine a situation in which a shipment is due at 5:00 p.m. on Friday evening and that the person receiving the shipment has clearly stated that if the shipment is not on the trucks at that time, the order will be canceled. Now, further imagine that this shipment relies on a conveyor belt traversing four floors and that it breaks down at 4:15 p.m. The person we are looking for in that situation is not only the person who can fix the conveyor belt but also a person who can see alternative ways of getting the job done. Not only will this person need to see how to do things differently, but this individual may not be the manager or person in charge.

Companies are searching for individuals and organizational structures where employees are able to find creative solutions, work cooperatively, and adopt different roles and functions, and problem solve as a way of life. Real-life performance is the test.

How well do schools prepare such learners described above? And to what extent does assessment play a role in creating flexible learners who trust in their own ability to solve unique problems? As Diane Ronis points out in this book, today's schools still largely rely on standardization through standardized testing. The landscape of learning looks very different in the twenty-first century, and corporations are frustrated and alienated by an educational system that relies on nineteenth-century learning.

But what does learning look like when it is not tied to what Whitehead (1979) calls "inert knowledge" and we call "surface knowledge"? In a rapidly changing world, learning means being able to live with paradox and ambiguity.

It also means constructing, not memorizing, answers. Real learning is almost always a deep struggle involving the adjustment of beliefs and assumptions and inevitably engages issues of identity. Real learning is deeply personal. It requires that learners participate meaningfully in the ideas and subjects that they explore as they shape and reshape what they know and want to know. It requires that learners learn from genuine feedback.

But how do we understand such learning? How do we create it in our schools? And most important of all, how do we measure it? Diane Ronis has written an intelligent book that brings coherence and intelligence to understanding how to assess such learning.

She has framed her conclusions, to some extent, on a perspective based on a set of 12 learning principles that consolidate what is known of learning theory and include implications from the neurosciences.

The principles, as a whole, strongly suggest that learning is far more holistic, integrated, and complex when it occurs in real-life contexts. Learning includes the emotions, cognition, the context, the search for meaning, and conscious and unconscious processes, among others. The state of mind of the learner (including assumptions, conceptual frameworks) and beliefs all interact with learning.

Armed with this background, Diane takes on the task of assessment. She emphasizes that the learner needs to participate in the evaluation process and the need for what we call "active processing." Often teachers who teach through experiences and who create an empowered learning community forget, or do not know how, to help students consolidate skills and knowledge that were gained during the experience. Such consolidation is process oriented and critical for continued and future learning.

The book also includes up-to-date thinking grounded in the field of assessment itself, such as the development of rubrics, portfolio assessment, and teaching for high standards. The author ties all of these elements to teaching examples. Diane demonstrates clear knowledge of what happens in classrooms all over this country and leads educators willing to take a leap in teaching and assessment.

We predict that what will happen, if educators follow her lead, is that teaching and assessment will become part of the students' learning as they learn from everything, including their own mistakes and corrections. They will pass standardized tests but will find such tests extremely limited and even embarrassing given what they can actually do.

When that happens, schools will have aligned themselves with the challenges and opportunities that life in an interconnected global world calls for.

—*Renate Nummela Caine, PhD*

Preface

The logic of it all, or lack thereof, continues to elude me. After years of hard scientific data containing the potential to revolutionize the way teaching and instruction are carried out, our educational system struggles to stop revolving in the same old circles. While it has been implied by the findings of neuroscience that the brain's true learning potential is actually thwarted and mishandled through the use of traditional instruction methods that fragment and dehumanize learning, we too frequently see these methods employed. These conundrums challenge the best teachers and schools to lead their learning communities to better practices that respect the natural learning processes of students. Likewise, questions are raised by students in my university education classes. My students, after being schooled in the logic of brain-compatible learning, frequently find in the field that they are required to use textbooks that cover too many learner outcomes, and employ worksheets to reinforce this "learning." The explanation for the disconnects most probably lies with the pressure on teachers and schools, in spite of what scientific research has indicated to be best for students, to "teach to the test."

Our nation continues to languish in the midst of a crisis of accountability. The No Child Left Behind Act of 2001 has not helped. By emphasizing test results at the expense of true comprehension, students are being taught via methods that exacerbate the very problem that dedicated educators have been striving so hard to correct.

Standardized testing goes back to the early twentieth century when the perceived need for a certain measure of objectivity in assessment gave rise to the "scientific testing movement." The result of this movement was the standardized test: a mass-produced, multiple-choice examination that could be administered to large numbers of individuals with consistent results. The standardized test became the assessment tool of choice for monitoring school quality and continues to drive the machine that prevents us from realizing student potential. Our current testing environment originates with a laudable national determination to make education more equitable and close the gap between high and low achievers, particularly for identified student populations that experience lower success than others. The intent was to shine a bright light of accountability that would require that all students be taught well and in ways that they could learn. Unfortunately, when schools are held captive to tests as the sole measure to quantify learning according to standardized norms and that sort students according to their abilities to memorize disconnected facts and algorithms, true learning cannot flourish.

As good teachers and learners know, real and enduring knowledge is much more than an ability to manipulate a mathematical formula out of context or recognize a list of word definitions. Real learning is about the learner's ability to apply learned skills to real-life, contextual settings. True understanding is best represented by the learner's ability to solve unfamiliar problems that have no clear-cut, neat answers, problems that are unpredictable and that entail an ability to extrapolate from existing knowledge to create novel and unique solutions.

Measurement of the development of such knowledge in students cannot be ascertained through traditional assessment methods alone. To rely on large-scale, standardized tests as the single, most important indicator of learning progress is to put us at risk of lagging behind our global counterparts. Each child, like a snowflake, is a unique individual with his or her brain preferring a particular learning style, possessing an array of intelligences, as well as sets of both learned and innate abilities. If each one of them is so singular, we cannot rely entirely on a "one-size-fits-all" assessment method.

If assessment and "teaching to the test" are what drives the educational system, then it is time to make assessment the place to begin the motion of change. Educators can consistently balance required standardized assessments with ongoing alternative assessment methods that are compatible with the way the brain learns and contain and employ rigorous standards and high challenge levels. Only then can veteran and fledgling teachers alike initiate the changes needed to educate our students to be successful citizens in the twenty-first century.

—*Diane Ronis*

Introduction

THE BRAIN AND ASSESSMENT CONNECTION

The publication of the report *A Nation at Risk* in 1983 made it clear that the United States was experiencing a crisis within its educational system. The purpose of the commission's inquiry was to analyze the "quality" of education in the United States, as it then existed. The unplanned result, however, was to initiate dramatic changes in traditional public education and provoke a national preoccupation with quantifying educational achievement and assessing accountability (National Commission on Excellence in Education, 1983).

Many of the current methods for assessing accountability are inconsistent with what educators and researchers believe works to improve learning and comprehension. The standards movement, which began in the late 1980s, serves as a good example. While high standards for all students is a worthy goal, assessment and evaluation of those standards are often done in a way that does not support learning that is enduring.

A parallel exploration during recent years has been brain research that has focused on new theories of the way in which the human brain acquires new knowledge. Many of these learning theories seem to suggest that traditional instruction methodologies actually operate in a way that undermines the brain's natural learning style. This learning style, according to the National Research Council's recent educational and neuroscientific research appears to indicate the following:

1. The functional organization of the brain and the mind depend upon and benefit positively from experience.

2. Development is not merely a biologically driven unfolding process, but also an active process that derives essential information from experience.

3. Some experiences have the most powerful effects during specific sensitive periods, whereas others can affect the brain over a much longer time span.

In other words, the way we learn is through firsthand experience. No other method is as effective as the hands-on activities through which the individual experiences and assimilates new information. The implication here is that for curriculum to be effective, it must be addressed in terms of its relevance or meaning for the students. Content and instruction must function within a meaningful context if they are to result in learning that lasts. In other words, instruction and assessment are most compatible with the brain's natural processes when they move away from earlier practices in which information is taken out of context, such as when mathematics is taught through the use of specific numerical examples showing students solution algorithms. In this mode, such teacher-centered demonstrations are then following by the students completing large numbers of similar problems on their own (Ronis, 2001).

Improving education quality then, requires an array of changes focusing on attitudes, practices, and training. By focusing on the memorization of isolated skills and facts rather than inquiry and discovery involving connections and comprehension of underlying concepts, much of American education has been organized for frustration. Many students, nevertheless, learned the ropes and survived, and many teachers instinctively made learning come alive with real experiences. Now, with findings emerging from neuroscience that have implications for teaching, we are able to make learning and assessment more natural for all students. In brain-compatible classrooms, students are offered the kinds of learning experiences that teach knowledge organization, information synthesis, reinforcement of self-correction skills, and concept application. Such learning experiences demonstrate and employ the contextual application of new knowledge in much the same way these applications occur in real life, imbuing the content learning with relevancy and connection to the world outside the classroom. Brain-compatible learning focuses on solutions to problems that require reasoning rather than the repetitious memorization of bits of information. While all students should be held to rigorous standards, some may, indeed, need to achieve these goals through different and perhaps unconventional ways. In other words, the most effective teachers today teach not only content but also understanding of that content by incorporating research into practice.

ORGANIZATION OF THE BOOK

Brain-Compatible Assessments is presented in six chapters, each of which is summarized here.

Chapter 1: The Assessment Revolution examines the history and reforms in the field of evaluation and assessment and calls for a new paradigm. It discusses the No Child Left Behind Act of 2001 and the implications of this legislation. It explains what kinds of reforms are needed and how such reforms can change the face of future assessment.

Chapter 2: Assessment Formats: Standards, Design, and Brain-Compatible Learning focuses on the development, implementation, and assessment of student work. It details how to design valid brain-compatible assessments and explains why assessments that support metacognitive processing and collaborative project work also support brain-based learning.

Chapter 3: Multiple Intelligences and Brain-Compatible Assessment focuses on the implications of MI theory on standards and assessment and why this theory is so brain compatible.

Chapter 4: Instruction and Assessment discusses implications for connected learning and assessment from neuroscientific findings and what these findings might mean for education in general; how the standards dialogue influences brain-compatible learning and vice versa.

Chapter 5: Wiring the Curriculum: Standards and Their Technological Applications deals with technology and implications for brain-compatible education. Included are discussions relating to classroom computer use, software selection, and navigating the Internet.

Chapter 6: Collaborative Learning examines the most highly brain-compatible of the instructional strategies.

The Glossary, at the back of the book, contains frequently used terms and their definitions. Each glossary term appears in bold on its first mention in the book.

Each of the six chapters provides three OPPORTUNITIES FOR ASSESSMENT that provide a complete view of a fully integrated assessment process and are designed as follows.

OPPORTUNITY FOR ASSESSMENT

TITLE

Level

Elementary, Middle, or Secondary, with suggestions for modifications to accommodate other levels.

Content Standards

Standards drawn from various national association standards such as those of the National Council of Teachers of Mathematics (NCTM) and the National Council of Teachers of English/International Reading Association (NCTE/IRA) and include standards from at least two disciplines. Suggestions for adaptations to other content areas are also provided.

Performance Standards

"Contextualize" content standards by identifying the manner in which they must be demonstrated and their expected level of performance or understanding.

Multiple Intelligences and Learning Styles

Verbal, Visual, Logical, Musical, Interpersonal, Intrapersonal, Bodily, Naturalist. Based on the concept of teaching to student strengths; therefore, performance tasks exercise a number of the intelligences.

Performance Task

Each unique task, while briefly stated, conforms to the 12 brain/mind learning principles laid out by Caine, Caine, McClintic, and Klimek (2004) and accomplishes the following:

- Provides variety and stimulation
- Encourages students to create products using their creative interests as the springboard
- Follows either the "small group" or "pair and share" model, allowing for greater use of individualized learning plans that reflect distinctive learning styles, assorted intelligences, strengths, interests, and needs
- Has the teacher acting as the resource, facilitator, coach, and/or guide

Assessment Technique

Rubrics, Observations, Student Self-Assessment, and Portfolios are used. Each assessment technique is geared to best measure the particular performance task. Student performance samples are also offered where appropriate to illuminate expectations and to demonstrate what "excellence" should look like.

Through the use of the OPPORTUNITIES FOR ASSESSMENT like the ones included in this book, students will discover that learning need not consist of the memorization of information having little or no application to their lives. Rather, they will be able to observe how high-quality learning and comprehension really involve exploration, discovery, conjecture, and relevance, based on rigorous yet authentic subject matter content. Teachers will find that assessments, when ongoing and brain compatible, are indeed opportunities—opportunities for success.

To begin your journey toward establishing brain-compatible assessment in your classroom, try taking this self-evaluation quiz before reading the book. (Rate your current classroom learning climate to see where you may want to start.)

SELF-EVALUATION INTERPRETATION

Odd-numbered questions run counter to brain-compatible instructional strategies, whereas even-numbered problems support such strategies. The higher the number of "frequently" answers chosen for odd-numbered problems, the more the reader will want to focus on even-numbered strategies to bring his or her classroom in line with brain-compatible assessment.

Learning and Assessment Climate Self-Evaluation:

Is the Environment in Your Classroom Conducive to Brain Compatible Learning and Assessment?

		Never	Occasionally	Frequently
1	I use letter or number grades for evaluation purposes.			
2	I use written feedback comments in my evaluations.			
3	I introduce new concepts and ideas as isolated and separate content areas.			
4	I introduce new concepts by connecting them to previous concepts.			
5	The questions/problems that I use in my classroom ask for single answers or solutions paths.			
6	The questions/problems that I use in my classroom make use of multiple solutions paths (correct solutions may differ).			
7	Students learning differences get in the way of instruction and assessment.			
8	I pay attention to students' different learning styles.			
9	My instruction directly follows the text.			
10	I connect my instruction and assessment to student interests and/or experiences.			
11	In my class, students' motivation is guided by external rewards and punishments (grades).			
12	In my class, student incentive is guided by intrinsic motivation (student satisfaction with accomplishment).			
13	I use lecture and other teacher-centered strategies.			
14	I use cooperative learning groups and other student-centered strategies.			
15	I find I am pressured to teach, test, and move on.			
16	I spend planning time with colleagues to examine student work and assessment products.			

Publisher's Acknowledgments

Corwin Press gratefully acknowledges the contributions of the following reviewers:

Christelle Estrada, PhD
Director of Professional Development Services and Secondary School Support
Salt Lake City School District
Salt Lake City, UT

Mike Lindstrom, PhD
Office of Research, Evaluation and Testing
Anoka-Hennepin Schools
Coon Rapids, MN

Vicki Edwards, EdD
Director of Student Achievement and Assessment
Deer Valley Unified School District
Phoenix, AZ

Jenni Gibbs
Literacy Coordinator
Deer Valley Unified School District
Phoenix, AZ

About the Author

 **Diane Ronis** is currently a professor of education at Southern Connecticut State University and holds a PhD in Curriculum and Instruction. She has been involved in the field of education since 1968, and has been a keynote speaker and presenter at numerous conferences and workshops throughout the country. Her area of expertise is in the transferring of neuroscientific research into practical strategies that classroom teachers can easily implement.

As a new professor in 1998, she began creating material for her classes that would be in keeping with her vision for cutting-edge, high-quality instruction and assessment methodologies teachers would find easy to understand and implement. These materials evolved into the five books she has published: *Clustering Standards in Integrated Units* (2002), *Critical Thinking in Math* (2002), *Problem-Based Learning for Math & Science: Integrating Inquiry & the Internet* (2001), *Brain-Compatible Assessments* (2000; second edition 2007), and *Brain-Compatible Mathematics* (1999; second edition 2007).

The Assessment Revolution

U.S. educators have been thrown into a score-boosting game they cannot win. More accurately, the score-boosting game cannot be won without doing educational damage to the children in our public schools.

—W. James Popham (2001, p. 12)

THE NEED FOR CHANGE

There is a growing recognition that, in spite of a recent rise in standardized test scores, students are not necessarily becoming better educated or more knowledgeable. The discrepancy between traditional **testing** results and the reality of what high school students know and can or cannot do provoked disenchantment with traditional methods of assessing student learning and has given impetus and momentum to the authentic **assessment** movement. While grades are here to stay in most districts, and state and national tests will continue to constitute a powerful external force in our school environments, what teachers and schools can do for the benefit of students is to counterbalance these standardized assessments with ongoing meaningful, authentic assessments of student understanding. An assessment focus that de-emphasizes traditional grades and demystifies the entire grading process is more in line with the manner in which the brain learns new information. Most advocates of authentic assessment do not want to totally eliminate traditional tests. What they seek is a good mix of assessment practices.

Cream of the Crop

Who is expected to learn? The central purpose for schooling has been reflected in this question. Historically, education has sorted and selected students much like separating cream from milk. While the "cream" was destined for higher education, the "milk" became the workforce required to power the industrial economy. Consequently, policies, practices, programs, and procedures were developed in which all students were taught the same way (the teacher lecturing to passive students), given the same amount of time, and tested with assessments based on the **bell-shaped curve.** The system manufactured a large common labor force with workers identified by their failure to achieve.

A system whose main purpose is sorting and selecting is at odds with the concept of educating all students. Outrage at the inequity of a stratified and stratifying education system was what propelled the legislation of the No Child Left Behind Act of 2001 (NCLB) and accounts for its overwhelming support from both political parties. The sad irony has been that the emphasis on testing and the practice of "teaching to the test" that the legislation has produced have undercut the values of the original intention. Brain-compatible, standards-based education introduces an orientation for ensuring that no child is left behind that is focused specifically on sustained achievement for all students—regardless of gender, race, ethnicity, or socioeconomic status. Given appropriate time, multiple and varied instructional strategies, and clear goal expectations, many of the students previously considered underachievers (the "milk") can now meet or exceed rigorous academic standards.

THE STANDARDS

The National Commission on Excellence in Education's now famous report *A Nation at Risk* sparked, or at least rekindled, the standards movement in America. Educational practices and policies had brought about what the report called "unilateral educational disarmament" (National Commission on Excellence in Education, 1983, p. 5). In an attempt to "re-arm" America's youth, a system driven by standards was sought. The Education Summit in 1989, called for and attended by then-president George H. W. Bush and the nation's governors, set the stage for the establishment of national standards. The National Council of Teachers of Mathematics (NCTM) soon developed a set of goals that were very well received. Other subject-area organizations followed NCTM's lead and developed national standards of their own. The National Education Standards and Improvement Council (NESIC) was created in 1994 as part of the Goal 2000 legislation to "oversee and certify" standards created by the states (Kendall & Marzano, 1996).

Soon however, the enthusiasm for standards waned. **Content standards** in some areas had sparked controversy, and the sheer size and complexity of the standards produced were overwhelming. In addition, by 1995 the NESIC had effectively ceased to function. The standards movement was down but not out. The re-authorization of the Elementary and Secondary Education Act (now known as the Improving America's Schools Act [IASA]) in 1994 reinvigorated the standards dialogue by mandating the establishment of standards for schools receiving federal funds. By January 1998, 38 states had drafted academic standards in core subjects (English, math, science, and social studies) and 34 states used standards-based assessments of math and English. However, scholars engaged by the Thomas B. Fordham Foundation found that only one state had truly rigorous and clear standards in English, one in history, three in geography, three in math, and six states in science. A consistently rigorous level of standards in content area is a requirement if U.S. education is to step back from the precipice of risk. For educational reform based on standards to be successful, it must be consistent with brain-compatible instructional methodologies.

NCLB (2001), the most recent iteration of the Elementary and Secondary Education Act of 1965 (ESEA), introduced the issue of accountability. According to the U.S. Department of Education, accountability is a crucial step in addressing the achievement gaps that are perceived to exist. Under NCLB, every state is required to (1) set standards for grade-level achievement and (2) develop a system to measure the progress of all students and subgroups of students in meeting those state-determined, grade-level standards.

In effect, however, what NCLB has done is put an unreasonable emphasis on high-stakes test results, forcing teachers to forgo "meaningful and relevant" instructional methodologies in favor of a test-prep curriculum. Such high-stakes, statewide achievement tests do not measure the vast amount of curricula set forth by states and school districts. These tests tend to measure those things that are easy to measure, in an efficient and economical way. This means that the focus is on lower-order thinking skills, with a sprinkling of higher-order skills, such as writing a short essay (Popham, 2003). The reality of this situation is that schools and teachers, faced with ever-increasing demands to avoid the "failing school" label, logically focus on the curriculum content that is most likely to improve test scores, the unfortunate result being the narrowing of our nation's curriculum.

Writing and the ability to express oneself and one's environment are essential to literacy. Journal writing works with the processes of the brain and therefore stimulates understanding. The OPPORTUNITY FOR ASSESSMENT #1 is presented as a stimulus for introspection and cross-content knowledge integration. While creative writing has traditionally been a part of language arts instruction, creativity and writing are valuable in promoting student understanding of other content areas. When journals are used in multidisciplinary situations, they help build specialized vocabulary and a deeper understanding of underlying concepts. Students can keep a science fiction writing journal where the concepts experienced in the lab can be synthesized into an environment of the students' own making (a science fiction story). Or, students might engage in a historical diary project where they imagine themselves in the position of an historical figure, writing from that person's perspective.

The Creative Writing Journal is appropriate for students of every level as long as the performance criteria are appropriately adapted. Even emergent readers and writers can take part with the assistance of a "scribe" or a voice-activated word-processing program or tape recorder.

OPPORTUNITY FOR ASSESSMENT #1

Creative Writing Journal

Level Secondary

Content Standards

Language Arts: National Council of Teachers of English/International Reading Association (NCTE/IRA)

- ❑ Students adjust their use of spoken, written, and visual language (e.g., conventions, style, and vocabulary) to communicate effectively with a variety of audiences and for different purposes.
- ❑ Students employ a wide range of strategies as they write and use different writing process elements appropriately to communicate with different audiences for a variety of purposes.
- ❑ Students apply knowledge of language structure, language conventions (e.g., spelling and punctuation), media techniques, figurative language, and genre to create, critique, and discuss print and nonprint texts.

Multiple Intelligences and Learning Styles

- ❑ Visual/Spatial
- ❑ Logical/Mathematical
- ☑ Verbal/Linguistic
- ❑ Musical/Rhythmic
- ❑ Bodily/Kinesthetic
- ❑ Interpersonal/Social
- ☑ Intrapersonal/Introspective
- ❑ Naturalist

Performance Task

Over the course of a semester, students will maintain a personal creative writing journal in which they free-write for a half hour every day.

Assessment Technique

Portfolio creation; the journal itself serves as the portfolio. Only Novice (work is of poor quality) and Proficient (work is of satisfactory quality) are given because, in this instance, it is not what is being written that is being evaluated, but the fact that writing has taken place (see Figure 1.1).

Journal Assessment Rubric

Qualities Evaluated	Proficient Excellent and proficient work quality	Novice Beginning-level work quality
Effort	Journal entries for most days. Substantial material presented in each entry.	No journal entries for most days. Length of entries is insubstantial.
Individual Progress	Progress evident from first entry to last.	No progress evident from first entry to last.

Figure 1.1

FORMS OF ASSESSMENT

The educational system is now presented with the challenge of developing appropriate and meaningful ways to evaluate the extent to which students are meeting the standards. Time-honored methods, such as the standardized test, are being called into question. More progressive, brain-compatible methods of measurement are gaining favor in light of scientific information about ways in which the brain might be processing information. An example of how a **rubric** can be used to assess with a deeper view into a wide range of student performances can be seen in Figure 1.1. Such a rubric also provides a guide for assessment-driven instruction and a transparent guide for students that allows teachers to clearly communicate to learners the measures of success and allows students to monitor their own progress.

The Standardized Test

Horace Mann, the father of public education in the United States, was a firm believer in the concept of testing. As early as 1845, Mann was advocating the use of written tests comprising large numbers of questions with set answers as a way to evaluate student performance. Even then, early research in assessment and **evaluation** revealed problems with the objectivity of such evaluations. In further studies, it was discovered that when different teachers were given the same tests to grade, the scores varied widely and bore no relation to any uniform set of standards. In other early studies, papers that had received passing grades from evaluators the first time were graded as failures when given to the same evaluators a second time, with the reverse situation occurring with as much frequency (Hart, 1994).

The results brought attention to the need for greater objectivity in assessment. In fact, it was the perceived need for objectivity that first gave rise to the scientific testing movement early in the twentieth century. The direct result of the movement was the development of the standardized test, a mass-produced, multiple-choice test that could be administered to large numbers of persons with consistent results. To ensure the accuracy of the tests, statistical concepts and techniques were designed and developed to eliminate problems like subjectivity in scoring. By 1928, there were over a thousand standardized tests available in the United States, each with a statistically calculated measure of the test's validity (how well it measures what it is supposed to measure) and reliability (how consistently the scoring results will be over time and in different testing situations). The development of the standardized test led to the rise of the testing industry whose market expanded in the 1920s with the onset of official state testing. After World War II, two main trends contributed to the further expansion of the test industry: the decline of the one-room schoolhouse and accountability. By 1950, the one-room schoolhouse had evolved into a new model of instruction, one based on the factory design with its concept of mass production. The secret to making this factorylike schoolwork was to break the learning down into small skills and bits of knowledge that could be taught and learned sequentially as the students moved along the educational assembly line. Standardized tests fit nicely into this model of instruction. With their multiple-choice formats, standardized tests made the perfect tool for measuring the mastery of subskills, or bits of content, for large numbers of students. With the advent of computerized scoring, standardized tests became even cheaper and easier to use.

The second trend that encouraged the growth of the test industry was the increasing concern over accountability. During the postwar years, baby boomers swelled school populations, and the amount of money that was spent on education increased precipitously. Unfortunately, student achievement did not keep pace with the educational investment. By the 1970s, Scholastic Aptitude Test (SAT) scores began falling while employers started complaining that high school graduates were neither able to read nor write. Angry taxpayers, not quite sure of where to place the blame for the failure, sought solutions by measuring and monitoring what went on in the schools. As a result, the standardized test became the assessment tool of choice for monitoring school quality.

By the 1980s, educators had begun to realize that the standardized test was fast becoming the driving force behind the curriculum. The consensus among many educators was that to move education away from its emphasis on memorization of isolated facts, education would need to move in a direction of increased emphasis on higher cognitive thinking skills. For such a change to take place, assessment methods needed to evolve and be redesigned into something other than the machine-scored multiple-choice test. With NCLB (2001) however, the politicized pendulum was demonstrating a return to those much-maligned standardized tests, to the chagrin of most educators.

Technically Speaking

Standardized tests usually fall into two categories: norm-referenced and criterion-referenced tests. Both test types rely heavily on the multiple-choice format. Norm-referenced standardized test scores give numbers that reflect achievement and performance of isolated skills at a particular moment in time. The norm-referenced testing is designed as a means of ascertaining an individual's performance in relation to the performance of other individuals on the same test. The scores are plotted along some form of the normal distribution curve. Such a test is designed to show how a given student or group of students rank when compared with other test takers of the same age and grade. With this method of evaluation, a certain percentage of the tested population must fail to establish the norm against which all the other students are measured. In a standardized test, the norm (or standard of performance) is determined by recording the scores of a large group, such as a sample of elementary school students. When subsequent students take the test, the norms for them will be those of the larger group (the group on which the test was "standardized"). Figure 1.2 shows a normal distribution curve. Test items are selected based on their ability to make distinctions among students. Items on which most students score either very high or very low are not retained for future tests because they do not discriminate among students. Consequently, some content standards may not be measured.

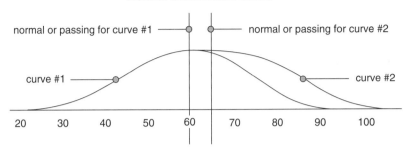

Figure 1.2

A criterion-referenced test, on the other hand, is a way to measure an individual's performance against established criteria or expected standards (what a student should know at a given point in his or her education). The goal is to help all students attain at least the minimum level of mastery. Items chosen for inclusion on such tests are intended to reveal a student's strengths and weaknesses in terms of knowledge or skills. Competency tests and achievement tests are types of criterion-referenced tests. The criterion-referenced approach specifically provides for the following:

1. Test takers know what level of performance is expected of them in advance; therefore, students know what they must do to be successful on assignments and tests.

2. Teacher's subjective judgment is limited because the test content is not decided by a single individual.

3. Students are not fighting against each other for a place on the distribution curve; consequently, a noncompetitive environment results.

The problem with criterion-referenced tests from a brain-compatibility perspective is that the items chosen may be measuring only superficial knowledge, involving memorization and mechanics rather than higher-order thinking skills. In addition, because the evaluation occurs in an environment foreign to the subjects' context, is stressful, and occurs only once, it cannot give an accurate portrayal of an individual's knowledge.

Critics point out that standardized tests corrupt the very process they seek to improve. America's reliance upon tests, they contend, has damaged teaching and learning by putting too much value on memorization of isolated bits of information at the expense of higher thinking skills. Teachers often feel the pressure to focus more on what can be easily tested than on what is important for students to learn. Students are thereby conditioned to be passive learners who can only recognize information rather than construct their own answers and solutions.

In addition, standardized testing neglects the vital aspect of emotion in assessment. (For a discussion of the role emotion plays in the learning process, see the "Emotion in Context" section of Chapter 4.) If a student typically learns in a classroom and then is tested in a media center or an auditorium, that student is more likely to underperform. Similarly, if a student learns in a particular emotional state, he or she will most readily recall that learning when in that same state. It is the job of the assessor to match the memory mechanism at assessment time to that which occurred during learning, or the student may not be as successful as he or she might be in demonstrating the knowledge learned. The best way to do such an evaluation is by providing opportunities for assessment that occur as part of the learning process.

Observation and conferencing strategies work very well for tasks that have some kinesthetic or performance element to them where progress toward a goal can be monitored in addition to assessing the final product. OPPORTUNITY FOR ASSESSMENT #2 has students acting out a kind of interplanetary play. Planets in Motion offers a performance task appropriate to the elementary level. (Pre–K students may also be able to learn from and enjoy this activity.) In addition, middle-level students can perform the task with a higher degree of accuracy and "reality" by plotting the respective planets' orbits and scaling them down to fit on the playground. They may also be asked to reflect upon the role size plays in the gravitational pull of an object and why planets travel in elliptical orbits. Secondary-level students may act out more complex processes or re-create famous experiments "live" in front of an audience. These performances can be videotaped and used by students to critique their individual performances, or the tapes can stand as example for future classes of what excellence looks like. Activities in which students play a particular role in a complex process must allow time for students to see their role as part of a bigger picture, otherwise learning may be fragmented. Witnessing their performance on videotape or seeing their place on a diagram of their creation will help them bring their experiences into the larger context.

Observation Rubric

Focus Items	Observations
Concepts: planet placement in the solar system	Jimmy has difficulty locating Earth's position relative to the sun. Beth (as the sun) explained to Jimmy why he had to move around her.
Techniques: verbal interaction of students with teacher guidance	Some students are having difficulty with each planet's orbit and rotation speed. Design an activity that will help focus them on this concept.
Problem solving/reasoning	Some of the students are able to explain the logic of the solar system to the others. We need to go over the basic planet relationships in class again.
Communication and collaboration	Beth and Tom are very helpful with the other students, always trying to help them see where they might fit into the orbit design. Jimmy, as Earth, is set on being the center even though he knows his science facts.

Figure 1.3

OPPORTUNITY FOR ASSESSMENT #2

Planets in Motion

Level Elementary

Content Standards

Science

Content Standard D: Earth and Space Science

- ❑ Structure and properties of the Earth system
- ❑ Earth's history and cycles
- ❑ Earth in the solar system

Language Arts

- ❑ Adjusts use of spoken, written, and visual language (e.g., conventions, style, and vocabulary) to communicate effectively with a variety of audiences and for different purposes

Physical Education

- ❑ Demonstrates competency in many movement forms and proficiency in a few movement forms
- ❑ Applies movement concepts and principles to the learning and development of motor skills

Multiple Intelligences and Learning Styles

- ☑ Visual/Spatial
- ❑ Logical/Mathematical
- ☑ Verbal/Linguistic
- ❑ Musical/Rhythmic
- ❑ Bodily/Kinesthetic
- ❑ Interpersonal/Social
- ❑ Intrapersonal/Introspective
- ❑ Naturalist

Performance Task

In a large area such as a playground, students will take turns placing themselves in different locations as they act out the rotation of the planets and their orbits. Once back in the classroom, students will write a paragraph about the planetary relationships.

Assessment Technique

Performance assessment (informal observation). Observation is an important means of assessment integration. With observation, the teacher is able to monitor the learning process as it occurs within the group (see Figure 1.3).

Student Samples (see Figure 1.5)

Paragraph Assessment Rubric

CRITERIA EVALUATED	NOVICE BEGINNING 1 NOT YET	BASIC DEVELOPING 2 YES BUT	PROFICIENT ACCOMPLISHED 3 YES	ADVANCED EXEMPLARY 4 YES PLUS
COMPREHENSION				
Level of Comprehension	Weak demonstration of comprehension; vague and confusing	Inconsistent demonstration of comprehension; superficial	Solid and consistent demonstration of comprehension	Masterful demonstration of profound and sophisticated comprehension
THOUGHT ORGANIZATION				
Ideas Clearly Focused and Well Supported	Few ideas are focused or supported	Ideas are focused and supported in places, but lack consistency	Ideas are competent, focused, and well supported	Ideas are powerfully supported, consistently focused, perceptive, and comprehensive
DEMONSTRATION OF EFFECTIVE WRITING				
Organization	Writing is aimless and disorganized	Writing demonstrates simplistic organization	Writing demonstrates logical and competent organization	Writing demonstrates mature and sophisticated organization
Word Choice	Repetitive, dull, or incorrect word usage	Routine, simple word choices	Some word choices are sophisticated, while others are routine	Word choices are vivid and sophisticated yet natural
Sentence Fluency	Numerous awkward, run-on, and/or fragmented sentences, making reading difficult	Sentence structure is uneven	Writing demonstrates good control of sentence structure	Writing demonstrates powerful and sophisticated control of sentence structure
EVIDENCE OF CRITICAL THINKING				
Clarity of Thought Analysis	Thoughts are vague, nonspecific, and lack evidence of organization	Ideas are logical but not well analyzed	Several ideas are logical and have been well analyzed	Intuitive analysis, with clear and precise thought process throughout

Figure 1.4

Student Samples

Advanced	Proficient
For over science period, we went to the playground and pretended to be the planets in our solar system. Mr. Blank told us to try and rotate in our own orbits as if we were the real planets moving around the sun.	Today we played that we were the planets turning around the sun. We were turning in paths called orbits.
Basic	**Novice**
We went to the playground today and made beleave we were the planits. I wanted to be the second plant venis.	We play planet in yard. I play mercy. I go to sun.

Figure 1.5

ALTERNATIVE ASSESSMENTS

Alternative assessments are any and all assessments other than the standardized test–type assessments. A broad definition of alternative assessment includes any type of assessment in which a student creates a response to a question rather than choosing a response from a given list (as with multiple-choice, true/false, or matching). Some of the different alternative assessments include short-answer questions, essays, products, performances, oral presentations, demonstrations, exhibitions, and portfolios.

Standards found in NCTM's *Principles and Standards for School Mathematics* (2000) and the National Research Council's *National Science Education Standards* (1995) present a vision of assessment that is highly brain compatible in that it is ongoing and carried out in multiple ways. By listening to, observing, and talking with students, by asking students questions to help reveal their reasoning, by examining students' individual or group written and/or problem-solving work, teachers are able to develop a more accurate and valid picture of what students know and can do.

When conceived of and used in such a nonthreatening, brain-compatible manner, assessment provides teachers with the best way to gain valid insights into their students' thinking and reasoning abilities. Consequently, assessment becomes a powerful tool to help teachers monitor the effectiveness of their own teaching, judge the utility of the learning tasks, and consider when and where to go next in instruction. The focus is on high but achievable targets for students to meet rather than comparing student performance to the performance of other students. When information is shared with the students regarding precisely what they are expected to know and be able to do, students are able to meet or even exceed the standards.

Informal and Formative Assessments

Formative assessments consist of information, gathered by teachers mainly in their day-to-day classroom encounters with students, that registers students' internal processing of information, the development of student understanding, student-to-student interaction, and the discussion and revision of ideas. This process can take a variety of formats and is used to inform the teacher's instruction and pinpoint needs of the group and of individual students to support their learning progress. Assessment should be embedded in instruction, or in other words, integrated within the instruction. To evaluate the intangible processes taking place in the classroom, especially during group activities, teachers gain important information from observations. Observation is particularly important as a means of bringing about such integration of instruction and assessment. Through group as well as individual student observations, teachers are able to develop a sophisticated and complex picture of student learning. By using an observation time frame of 10 to 15 minutes, teachers can acquire the optimal perspective on group processes regarding topic content, social dynamics, or needed help. The Observation Rubric (see Figure 1.3) provides a sample of how teachers might officially record their assessment observations in an orderly and relatively objective manner. It is a good method for the organization of observations and helps to connect students to the learning content.

Another informal assessment method is to conduct active meetings with students either individually or in small groups. Such meetings, or conferences, can be brief (3 to 5 minutes) or longer if needed. It is often beneficial to give a particular student or group a specific assignment, such as exploring a problem, asking a peer for an explanation, or researching a similar topic, in order to provide a focus for student work. In this way, the next conference or observation held with that particular group or individual will provide the teacher with a good indication of the progress made by the group or individual. Focused, informal assessments help teachers keep up with students' varied progress rates and needs, which is especially important with more extensive projects.

Authentic Assessment

One of the major forms of alternative assessment is the authentic assessment. An assessment is considered to be "authentic" when it involves students in tasks that are worthwhile, significant, and meaningful (tasks that take into account that the search for meaning is innate in all humans); occurs over time (not just one day); is open-ended; and allows for students to demonstrate competence in a variety of ways. Such assessments involve higher-order thinking skills along with the use of a broad range of knowledge. In addition, authentic assessment demonstrates to the student exactly what it means to do excellent work by making explicit the standards by which that work will be evaluated. In this sense, authentic assessments are standard-setting assessment tools rather than standardized assessment tools.

Authentic assessments are brain compatible. When correctly designed, they emphasize learning and thinking, especially those higher-order thinking skills involved in problem solving. Authentic assessments comprise meaningful tasks that reflect real-life, interdisciplinary challenges; they present students with complex, ambiguous, open-ended problems and tasks that integrate their knowledge and skills. Such assessments usually culminate in student products

Standardized Tests vs. Brain-Compatible Assessment

Standardized Testing	Brain-Compatible Assessment
• results based on a mythical standard or norm, which requires that a certain percentage of children fail	• establishes an environment where each child has the opportunity to succeed
• pressures teachers to narrow their curriculum so that they can specifically concentrate on the test material	• allows teachers to develop meaningful curricula and assess within the context of that program
• emphasizes a single instance assessment, which has no relation to the learning taking place in the classroom	• assessment is ongoing throughout the unit of study, and provides an accurate picture of student achievement
• focuses on errors and mistakes rather than what has been accomplished	• puts the emphasis on student strengths rather than weaknesses
• focuses too much importance on single sets of data (i.e., test scores) in making educational decisions	• provides multiple sources of evaluation that give an in-depth view of student progress
• treats all students in a uniform way	• treats each student as a unique human being
• discriminates against some students because of cultural background and learning style	• provides the opportunity to eliminate cultural bias and gives everyone an equal chance to succeed
• regards instruction and assessment as separate activities	• regards instruction and assessment as being a single, integrated activity
• answers are final, there is no opportunity for reflection or revision	• engages the student in a continual process of self-reflection, learning, and feedback, as well as revision
• focuses on the "right" answer without regard for understanding	• deals with comprehension and the learning process as much as the final product
• inexpensive and easy to administer and grade	• more difficult to achieve consistent, objective scoring results
• often provides results that can be simplified to a single numerical score	• data cannot easily be simplified as a single number
• easy to compare and contrast different populations of students	• difficult to compare different student populations

Figure 1.6

or performances that recognize and value each student's multiple abilities, varied learning styles, and individual background. Calculators and dictionaries are necessary tools in the real world. If the job of educators is to prepare students to function in the real world, then students should be taught when and how to use real-world tools. Therefore, calculators, dictionaries, relevant textbooks, and other materials should be made available to students during an evaluation if the evaluation is genuinely authentic.

To be brain compatible, authentic assessments must have the following qualities:

Structure

- Involve an audience, are more public than traditional forms of assessment
- Do not rely on arbitrary or unrealistic time constraints
- Contain questions or tasks that are known beforehand and are not "secret"
- Encompass multiple opportunities for demonstration of growth (i.e., portfolios) rather than one-time, stressful experiences
- Include some sort of collaboration with peers
- Allow for a significant degree of student choice

Intellectual Design Features

- Direct students toward more sophisticated uses of knowledge and skills (i.e., critical thinking skills)
- Integrate tasks and their outcomes
- Assess thinking processes rather than bits and pieces of isolated information
- May involve somewhat ambiguous or "messy" tasks and/or problems to be solved
- Utilize the student's own research or use of knowledge
- Present a challenge that emphasizes depth of knowledge and understanding
- Stimulate and educate so that students can learn from the assessment process

Grading and Scoring Standards

- Are based on clearly articulated criteria and **performance standards** rather than a curve or norm
- Use performance indicators, which allow students to know ahead of time what excellence looks like
- Make metacognitive activities such as self-assessment and self-reflection part of the total assessment process
- Use a multifaceted scoring system rather than a single numerical grade
- Demonstrate equity
- Identify hidden strengths rather than weaknesses
- De-emphasize competitive comparisons between students
- Allow for different learning styles, abilities, and interests

A STARTING POINT

The results of standardized norm-referenced tests have become the virtual standards by which American public education is judged. Standardized testing has its place, but it is ultimately a poor judge of a school's quality of instruction. Relevant and meaningful standards in conjunction with authentic assessments would provide a real means of evaluation. Any attempt to change the status quo, however, would first require that the validity of a new assessment strategy be quantified. A starting point for such would be the comparison of the performance of the same group of students on both the norm-referenced test and the replacement measure. Standards-based or criterion-referenced assessments can be cross-referenced to standardized norm-referenced tests by conducting a concurrent validity study (Burger & Burger, 1993). In such a study, students would complete both a standardized norm-referenced test and a criterion- or standards-based test measuring a similar domain, reading for example. Statistical analysis could then provide both correlated data and the relationship of performance standards to percentile scores. The linkage between the two assessments would assure that the new assessments are rigorous and that the performance standards are worthy. There is no one best assessment method; hence the flaw in NCLB. The choice of using multiple-choice tests, performances, projects, exhibitions, or portfolios depends on what is being assessed, the purpose for the assessment, and how the assessment results will be used. A combination and variety of assessment formats is what is needed for a thorough and complete picture of student progress and growth.

A project that takes a number of weeks to complete will, in theory, allow for greater student thought about the process and what they want their product to look like. Portfolio-type performance tasks, such as the one presented in OPPORTUNITY FOR ASSESSMENT #3, Campaign Scrapbook, allows students to choose the way in which they will depict an idea or concept. When left to choose, students will often pick depictions and activities that are best suited to their most pronounced learning styles. The end result of a campaign scrapbook will look different for each student, but the criteria upon which it is evaluated will remain the same. The organizational structure, for instance, may vary widely, but some organizational planning should be evident in the product. The scrapbook concept can be adapted to suit additional content areas and levels. Elementary students can create a scrapbook of food labels and remark upon the use of color, wording, and logos to introduce or reinforce the concept of the symbolic use of language. Secondary students might keep the campaign element of the scrapbook but include editorials along with campaign ads to compare and contrast the approaches, the purpose, and the relative effectiveness of each. Student can then reflect upon the concept of rhetoric and debate. An extension of the task at all levels can include students creating their own advertisements (or product labels).

OPPORTUNITY FOR ASSESSMENT #3

Campaign Scrapbook

Level Middle

Content Standards

Social Studies: National Council for the Social Studies (NCSS)

Individuals, Groups, and Institutions

- ❑ Social studies programs should include experiences that provide for the study of interactions among individuals, groups, and institutions.
- ❑ In schools, this theme typically appears in units and courses dealing with sociology, anthropology, psychology, political science, and history.

Power, Authority, and Governance

- ❑ Social studies programs should include experiences that provide for the study of how people create and change structures of power, authority, and governance.
- ❑ In schools, this theme typically appears in units and courses dealing with government, politics, political science, history, law, and other social sciences.

Language Arts

- ❑ Students read a wide range of print and nonprint texts to build an understanding of texts, of themselves, and of the cultures of the United States and the world; to acquire new information; to respond to the needs and demands of society and the workplace; and for personal fulfillment. Among these texts are fiction and nonfiction, classic and contemporary works.
- ❑ Students adjust their use of spoken, written, and visual language (e.g., conventions, style, and vocabulary) to communicate effectively with a variety of audiences and for different purposes.
- ❑ Students employ a wide range of strategies as they write and use different writing process elements appropriately to communicate with different audiences for a variety of purposes.
- ❑ Students apply knowledge of language structure, language conventions (e.g., spelling and punctuation), media techniques, figurative language, and genre to create, critique, and discuss print and nonprint texts.

Multiple Intelligences and Learning Styles

- ☑ Visual/Spatial
- ❑ Logical/Mathematical
- ☑ Verbal/Linguistic
- ❑ Musical/Rhythmic
- ❑ Bodily/Kinesthetic
- ❑ Interpersonal/Social
- ❑ Intrapersonal/Introspective
- ❑ Naturalist

Performance Task

Students will maintain a scrapbook of campaign advertisements from a variety of different candidates and chronicle alongside the ads their observations and reflections on those advertisements. Students can compare and discuss collected artifacts. This discussion can support individual learning and scaffold English language learners. In the case of the latter, some students may participate primarily at the level of collecting based on recognizable photos and names in headlines. This is an entry point to learning and group discussion, particularly with peer translating, where possible, to support their differentiated learning.

Assessment Technique

Portfolio Assessment is perhaps the best method to show a student's processing and reflection (see Figure 1.7). A rubric, such as the one in Figure 1.7, is a valuable portfolio assessment tool because it shows the student exactly where the artifact is strong and where it needs to be improved.

Campaign Scrapbook Evaluation Rubric

CRITERIA EVALUATED	NOVICE BEGINNING 1 NOT YET	BASIC DEVELOPING 2 YES BUT	PROFICIENT ACCOMPLISHED 3 YES	ADVANCED EXEMPLARY 4 YES PLUS
Organization	Poor organization with parts difficult to find or missing completely	Good organization, but not all parts included or not readily accessible	Well organized	Sophisticated organization; all parts included and readily accessible
Communication of Ideas	Ideas presented in a confusing manner	Some ideas communicated well, but others are confusing	All ideas clearly communicated	All ideas clearly communicated in a sophisticated and original manner
Comprehension (Insights and Connections)	Demonstrates little or no understanding	Some understanding demonstrated, but connections are limited	Clear connections demonstrated	Exceptional insight demonstrated by sophisticated connections
Variety	Little or no variety in ad choice	Some good ads included, but variety is limited	Good variety in choice of ads	Numerous high quality ads chosen from a wide variety of sources
Presentation	Insufficient effort is obvious; needs more work	Satisfactory presentation, but nothing to make it stand out	Attractive presentation catches audience attention	Creative and unique presentation; stands out from the rest
Reflection	Little or no evidence of reflective thought processes	Some insight evident, but inadequate effort	Evidence of insight and constructive thought	Mature, thorough, realistic, and constructive

Figure 1.7

Assessment Formats: Standards, Design, and Brain-Compatible Learning

Assessment focuses on gathering information about student achievement that can be used to make instructional decisions. Formative assessments provide opportunities for students to practice, take mental risks, learn from mistakes, and revise their work. They enable teachers to analyze student performance to date and provide targeted feedback for improvement.

—Carol Ann Tomlinson and
Jay McTighe (2006, p. 131)

ON THE LOOKOUT FOR SUCCESS

Evaluation is more than a single event. It is, instead, a complex process that shapes what one looks for in, and what can be said about, student performance. Typical tests, even challenging ones, tend to over-assess student knowledge and under-assess the application of that knowledge and true intellectual performance. Synthesis of knowledge, an ability that is rarely tested, cannot be assessed using multiple-choice tests because the demonstration of such synthesis requires the production of an original response that is unique to each student.

From a brain-compatible perspective, assessment is viewed as an ongoing activity in which teachers gather information about student learning in multiple ways: by listening, observing, talking with students, posing questions, and examining students' written work. Such means of assessment must be organized so that they can produce a coherent story of student progress, help students make more progress with greater focus, and complement other types of assessments. Helping students learn and grow becomes easier when day-to-day assessment is well integrated within the instruction process.

PERFORMANCE ASSESSMENTS

Performance assessments are brain compatible because they help learners make the connection between their instruction and the manner of assessment. Such integration also encourages intrinsic motivation, self-reflection, and responsibility on the part of the learner. When learners have also been carefully taught the criteria upon which their performance will be evaluated, and therefore know what will be expected of them, the assessment is not a highly stressful experience.

Performance assessments are composed of essentially two parts: the performance tasks and the performance criteria. Because different tasks require different sets of criteria, the task is designed first, employing the technique of "backward planning" (Wiggins & McTighe, 2005).

As one example of a performance task, timelines are a good way to assess student understanding of a broad concept and to see how the various "little pictures" make up the big one. The OPPORTUNITY FOR ASSESSMENT #4 challenges secondary-level students to construct a timeline showing the course of America's westward expansion. It requires an understanding of the many and various circumstances that propelled manifest destiny and requires that those occurrences be put into their proper context (their sequential places on a timeline continuum). Finding something's place in context is distinctly brain compatible and thus aids in student understanding and meaning making. Because paragraphs from textbooks must be distilled to their essence for inclusion on the chart, students must make choices about what events to include and be prepared to defend those choices. Different student teams may wish to depict westward expansion from different points of view (e.g., from a legislative perspective, a settler's perspective, a Native American perspective). Each depiction is unique and valid as long as the performance criteria and student reasoning are maintained. Timelines are visual representations that provide an adhesive quality to the work for students. Middle-level student performance tasks may not vary too widely from their secondary counterparts but should be tied to the appropriate content and performance standards. An elementary-level timeline project might require students to create a timeline of their own lives that contains their past, present, and predicted future. Artifacts from their lives (photographs, souvenirs, report cards, or a lock of hair) can be affixed to the timeline to for illustration.

To extend this early elementary example, teachers can ask students to learn about what is going on in the community or world, or learn about scientific discoveries during their lifetimes and add these events to their timelines to see a bigger context and connect to standards.

OPPORTUNITY FOR ASSESSMENT #4

Westward Expansion Timeline

Level Secondary

Content Standards

Social Studies: National Council for the Social Studies (NCSS)

Culture

❑ Social studies programs should include experiences that provide for the study of culture and cultural diversity.

Time, Continuity, and Change

❑ Social studies programs should include experiences that provide for the study of the ways human beings view themselves in and over time.

People, Places, and Environment

❑ Social studies programs should include experiences that provide for the study of people, places, and environments.

Language Arts: National Council of Teachers of English/ International Reading Association (NCTE/IRA)

❑ Students read a wide range of print and nonprint texts to build an understanding of texts, of themselves, and of the cultures of the United States and the world; to acquire new information; to respond to the needs and demands of society and the workplace; and for personal fulfillment. Among these texts are fiction and nonfiction, classic and contemporary works.

❑ Students apply a wide range of strategies to comprehend, interpret, evaluate, and appreciate texts. They draw on their prior experience, their interactions with other readers and writers, their knowledge of word meaning and of other texts, their word identification strategies, and their understanding of textual features (e.g., sound-letter correspondence, sentence structure, context, and graphics).

❑ Students adjust their use of spoken, written, and visual language (e.g., conventions, style, and vocabulary) to communicate effectively with a variety of audiences and for different purposes.

❑ Students conduct research on issues and interests by generating ideas and questions, and by posing problems. They gather, evaluate, and synthesize data from a variety of sources (e.g., print and nonprint texts, artifacts, and people) to communicate their discoveries in ways that suit their purpose and audience.

❑ Students use a variety of technological and information resources (e.g., libraries, databases, computer networks, and video) to gather and synthesize information and to create and communicate knowledge.

❑ Students use spoken, written, and visual language to accomplish their own purposes (e.g., for learning, enjoyment, persuasion, and the exchange of information).

(Continued)

Opportunity for Assessment #4 (Continued)

Multiple Intelligences and Learning Styles

☑ Visual/Spatial   ❏ Bodily/Kinesthetic
❏ Logical/Mathematical   ☑ Interpersonal/Social
☑ Verbal/Linguistic   ❏ Intrapersonal/Introspective
❏ Musical/Rhythmic   ❏ Naturalist

Performance Task

Working in pairs, students will create a timeline representing the chronology of the westward expansion of the United States. The timeline will be developed from research using primary sources and will contain corresponding graphics. The final version must clearly illustrate the sequencing of events so that students can identify patterns of cause and effect, which will be compared later to current situations.

Assessment Technique

Portfolio Creation—shows student progress over time; allows for extended product revision and development; a means for ongoing feedback between students and teacher (see Figure 2.1).

THE PERFORMANCE TASK

Performance tasks are the activities that students undertake (a performance, presentation, panel discussion, etc.) to demonstrate what they know and can do. Performance criteria are applied to those tasks for purposes of evaluation. For example, the creation of a graph is a task that provides the student with the opportunity to demonstrate accuracy, graphic representation, and organization. This, in turn, provides the teacher with the opportunity to judge the quality of the performance (the completed graph) by how well the student demonstrated his or her mastery of the criteria (in this case, accuracy, graphic representation, and organization). Both high-quality tasks and high-quality performance criteria are essential for the design of a good performance task assessment.

Performance Samples

Performance samples, the tangible products that serve as evidence of student achievement, can be created as an open-ended task, an extended task, or during portfolio creation. The open-ended task presents students with situations that encourage those of differing abilities and backgrounds to approach tasks in different ways and to follow multiple paths in the framing of their responses. The extended task is a long-term, multiple-goal project that might be assigned at the beginning of a term or unit of study. Such long-term projects often serve as the focal point for a unit of study. They create a real-world context for the learning and assessment by connecting content to a challenging and interesting task. Portfolio creation, a concept borrowed from artists and

Timeline Rubric

CRITERIA EVALUATED	NOVICE BEGINNING 1 NOT YET	BASIC DEVELOPING 2 YES BUT	PROFICIENT ACCOMPLISHED 3 YES	ADVANCED EXEMPLARY 4 YES PLUS
Content and Research Quality	Weak use of primary sources results in information presented out of sequence	Inconsistent quality of source material results in some segments being out of sequence	Accurate use of primary sources results in correctly sequenced presentation of events	Perceptive use of primary sources results in an explicitly sequenced and detailed presentation
Organization	Little or no logic, making the finished product difficult to understand	Some degree of logic evident	Logical format	Highly logical format makes finished product extremely easy to understand
Variety	Little or no variety evident	Some variety evident	Thoughtful and effective variety of graphics	Elegant timeline contains a wide variety of complex, colorful graphics
Communication	Confusing and difficult to understand	Some parts are more effectively communicated than others	Clear and easy to understand	Attention-getting appearance makes critical points stand out while entire product is easy to understand
Conventions	Numerous errors make reading difficult	Sufficient errors to distract reader	Most conventions correct with only occasional errors	Impeccable grammar, punctuation, and spelling throughout
Historical Perspective	Little or no evidence of understanding	Some evidence of understanding	Comprehension is clearly evident	Perceptive and sophisticated comprehension
Cause and Effect	Little or no clear evidence	Some evidence of patterns	Patterns are clearly identifiable	Patterns virtually "jump out"
Patterns in Event Sequencing	Little or no clear evidence of patterns in the timeline	Some patterns evident in event sequencing	Patterns in event sequencing are readily evident and clearly identifiable	Patterns of events appear to "jump out," drawing attention to the concept of cause and effect
Creativity and Originality	Dull and ordinary presentation	Innovative in some parts, but not consistent	Demonstrates innovation	Demonstrates uniqueness, innovation, and is aesthetically pleasing
Teamwork	Finished product displays very uneven contributions from team	Contributions from most of the team members evident	Finished product contains contributions from all team members	Finished product shows evidence of team synergy (whole is greater than the parts)

Figure 2.1

designers, has generated the most interest among authentic assessment enthusiasts and is discussed in detail below.

Portfolios

Portfolios are one of the most comprehensive means of evaluating learner growth and progress. A portfolio is an organized, purposeful collection of documents, artifacts (student work that goes into the portfolio), records of achievement (comments and observations by the teacher), and reflections (the student's personal thoughts on his or her own learning [**metacognition**]).

Types and Uses of the Portfolio

Among the variety of portfolio systems in use, three main types lend themselves most readily to education: the working portfolio, the showcase portfolio, and the assessment portfolio. The working portfolio is used to demonstrate a learner's growth over a period of time. It contains student works-in-progress as well as completed pieces. It is also where work can be stored until it is moved to either a showcase or assessment portfolio. This kind of portfolio provides a practical way for teachers to gain formative assessment information about individual students' progress toward success on any large independent project rather than allowing students to work independently and then find at the end they have not succeeded or not used their time well. The working portfolio is evaluated only periodically (if at all) to provide students with feedback, not a grade.

The showcase, or display portfolio (like those used by artists and other professionals) is used to demonstrate the highest level of achievement attained by an individual. Because it is a compilation of the learner's best work, it is also the portfolio method that best contributes to an individual's self-esteem.

The primary purpose of the third kind of portfolio, the assessment portfolio, is to document student learning regarding specific curriculum objectives. Items contained in this kind of portfolio are designed to demonstrate the learner's achievement of certain curriculum objectives.

Rationale for Use

Portfolios are not merely means for grading students, but rather, a means of assessing learning. Report cards usually provide only a single indication of performance, such as a letter or number grade. Portfolios, on the other hand, have the capability of providing a rich variety of performance descriptions.

The benefits of portfolios are that they accomplish the following:

1. Allow students to demonstrate significant learning through a finished product.

2. Provide parents with an opportunity to see and value students' progress.

3. Empower the teacher to become more knowledgeable about each student's strengths and weaknesses.

4. Encourage better one-on-one communication between the student and the teacher.

5. Enable the teacher to develop a more complete picture of each individual student to identify potential learning gaps before the end of a unit.

6. Promote both student and teacher awareness. (Students develop an awareness of their own learning styles and preferences while teachers are better able to assess the needs and wants of each student.)

7. Encourage the development of higher-order thinking strategies such as analysis, synthesis, and evaluation.

8. Value process as well as products.

Developing a Portfolio System

In view of the fact that portfolio entries represent a kind of performance, the steps involved in the development of an assessment portfolio system resemble the principles for developing good performance assessments.

1. **Curricular objectives** are determined.

2. Purpose (i.e., placement in an advanced class) is stated.

3. Performance tasks are outlined for the curricular objectives (encompassing both content and performance standards) to ensure that the tasks match the purpose or objectives of the instruction.

4. Criteria for each performance task are determined, and performance standards for each criterion are established ("backward planning").

5. Rubric is designed.

6. Evaluators are identified and trained to score the assessments (thereby enhancing reliability of the assessments).

Items placed in the portfolio must demonstrate and document what the students have learned. Assessment portfolios allow students to show aspects of their learning such as growth and progress, creativity and originality, and introspection, which are not well profiled in traditional assessments.

Developing the portfolio as an assessment tool requires careful planning and effort. A well-designed portfolio has the following characteristics:

Multisourced—A portfolio consists of numerous and varied components that can come in different forms (e.g., audiotapes, conference notes, photographs, computer disks, and artwork).

Authentic—The pieces included must be relevant and worthwhile.

Dynamic—A portfolio shows learning "in progress," the sequential development of a student's growth. The portfolio contains student-selected work taken from different aspects of that student's learning progress.

Explicit in purpose—The student must have a thorough understanding of the learning activity's purpose and a clear comprehension of the evaluation criteria and teacher expectations before any work is begun. This allows the student to better focus on what he or she is doing well and what needs improvement.

Well integrated—The student's work must have relevancy to the real world and his or her daily experiences. Skills should be taught and learned in context, addressing the "why" as well as "how" of the learning.

Student owned—The student learns to take responsibility for his or her own learning. Ultimately it is the student who chooses the work that will become the portfolio artifacts (evidence) and who is responsible for the feelings and information contained in the reflective self-evaluations.

Multipurpose—A portfolio can provide a link across grade levels and subjects when shared with other teachers.

In addition, a description statement is attached to each portfolio entry and specifies what the piece is, its purpose, and of what learning it demonstrates. The purpose of this descriptive statement is to help the student articulate his or her thoughts by providing a clear rationale for the inclusion of each item.

For a portfolio system itself to be successful, it must include five essential components:

1. Student Access: The students must always have free access to their portfolios. One of the goals of portfolio evaluation is that the students take responsibility of their own assessment, and without access, this cannot be achieved.

2. Student Ownership: Students must feel that they are in charge of their portfolio, not the teacher. It is up to the students to choose the items to be included as well as the method for the portfolio's organization.

3. Relevant Items: The work kept in the portfolio must be relevant to what the students have been doing in class and how they have grown as a result of that doing. Items included should demonstrate the kinds of changes the new learning has brought about.

4. Organization: With a portfolio collection as with any collection, there must be some kind of logical order and organization. A good organizational outline should include a student's statement about the portfolio's purpose and some means of tracking the contents (an entry log or table of contents).

5. Sharing: Students need the opportunity to share their work and their progress. Sharing makes students verbalize their reflections. In addition, the feedback provided from those with whom the material is shared allows for students to experience constructive criticism.

While the temptation is to focus primarily on the product (the portfolio), the development process is just as important because it integrates instruction and assessment. Figure 2.2 provides an overview of the Portfolio Assessment Process.

Implementation Strategies

At times, it may be necessary for the teachers to help students develop skills they will need to achieve a quality portfolio. The following are a sampling of possible implementation strategies teachers can use:

Summary of the Portfolio Assessment Process

Definition of Student Portfolios

- Systematic collection by students and teacher of multisourced student work
- Can be used to assess and evaluate student effort, improvement, learning processes, and achievement

Rationale for Portfolio Evaluation

- To provide a tangible record of a learner's development, growth, and progress or a concrete display of a learner's best work
- To provide a tangible display of the range of learning experiences and activities
- To encourage both student and teacher metacognitive thought through written reflection on learning goals, attitudes, knowledge, and strategies

Portfolio Contents

- Statement of purpose for portfolio
- Table of contents (compiled when prepared for presentation)
- Products or artifacts (student samples, tapes, photographs, copies of events or products, checklists, questionnaires, etc.)
- Written captions for each entry (description or explanation of each product or entry explaining the significance of each)

Advantages of Portfolios Over Tests

- Emphasis on both process and product
- Student involvement and ownership
- Open-ended and flexible, emphasizing the uniqueness of each learner
- Emphasis on goal setting and self-evaluation
- Rich and varied data on student growth taken at different developmental stages
- Supports self-assessment, goal-setting, and independent learning
- Portfolio components provide more concrete and relevant evidence of student growth than traditional assessments

How Do Portfolios Support Independent Learning?

- Can be used to showcase student's best work
- Encourage students to become actively involved in setting their own goals and objectives, as well as choosing which contents to showcase
- Reflections encourage metacognitive growth as well as higher cognitive levels of thinking such as analysis, synthesis, application, and evaluation

Figure 2.2

1. Provide a time and place for students to talk and write about their reactions to the new assessment process. Peer review of portfolio experience can be helpful to students as they learn to ask each other questions about the relative quality of the various portfolio components.

2. Encourage and support student attempts to make connections. Students may need reassurance that they will be able to experience success in an assessment system that emphasizes their responsibility for learning. Their self-esteem and motivation increase because they get credit for what they know instead of being penalized for what they don't know.

3. Empathize with the students' experience. Parts of this assessment process may be incomprehensible or overwhelming to the students when viewed from their perspective. Portfolio vocabulary and ideas may

be meaningless to them at first. It takes time to get these concepts across to them.

4. Be flexible in scheduling. The planning for activity completion must constantly be reevaluated and reexamined to provide responsible time for students to do their best work.

Projects that cause students to create something that can become visual reminders of a learning experience are in keeping with a brain-compatible perspective because learning is an ongoing process and because revisiting the portfolio artifacts will recall the learning experiences and strengthen long-term memory. OPPORTUNITY FOR ASSESSMENT #5 challenges students to create visual representations of the various geographic features of different regions of the United States. The performance task (creating the mobiles) provides an opportunity to evaluate student knowledge of geography. Geography Mobiles and all of the other assessment opportunities in this book do not call a halt to learning so that that learning can be measured. The proof of understanding is in the product. In this case, the product can hang in the classroom as a reminder of the concepts learned in that unit, providing a visual clue for students to recall the knowledge they demonstrated in constructing the mobiles. Parts of speech, geometry theorems, and chemical formulas also make for fine mobiles. Teachers should keep examples of the mobiles to show future classes. Students can be inspired by those who have gone before them and improve upon previous designs. If a group thinks of a way that they can improve their mobile, even after it's hung, teachers should allow them to make revisions as long as they continue to move forward with their new work.

PERFORMANCE CRITERIA

Good performance criteria help teachers and students understand the goals and target of the instruction. They help students know what is expected, what "excellence" looks like. Performance criteria also help teachers understand what kind of feedback is needed from students.

Teachers need to use different types of performance criteria to be assured of the validity and reliability of the assessment they construct. Three types of criteria are described below. *Product criteria* are used to assess the task outcome (the essay, performance, or project that students complete), while *process criteria* assess elements of the product (effort, homework, class participation). The third type is ***progress criteria***, which are used to assess a student's growth as he or she moves from level to level of accomplishment (from novice to proficient). Imagine assessing two students on an art project: One is a brilliant artist; the other has poor fine motor skills but is highly creative and always does her best. By using only product criteria (the appearance of the finished product), the second student may not be recognized for those things that she does well (effort). When process as well as progress criteria are part of the evaluation, fuller understanding of student achievement can be gleaned. All three of the performance criteria must be used to prevent inequities.

OPPORTUNITY FOR ASSESSMENT #5

Geography Mobiles

Level Elementary

Content Standards

Social Studies: NCSS

Culture

- ❏ Social studies programs should include experiences that provide for the study of culture and cultural diversity.
- ❏ In schools, this theme typically appears in units and courses dealing with geography, history, and anthropology, as well as multicultural topics across the curriculum.

Time, Continuity, and Change

- ❏ Social studies programs should include experiences that provide for the study of the ways human beings view themselves in and over time.

People, Places, and Environment

- ❏ Social studies programs should include experiences that provide for the study of people, places, and environments.

Language Arts: NCTE/IRA

- ❏ Students adjust their use of spoken, written, and visual language (e.g., conventions, style, and vocabulary) to communicate effectively with a variety of audiences and for different purposes.
- ❏ Students use spoken, written, and visual language to accomplish their own purposes (e.g., for learning, enjoyment, persuasion, and the exchange of information).

Visual Arts: National Art Education Association (NAEA)

- ❏ Understanding and applying media, techniques, and processes
- ❏ Using knowledge of structures and functions
- ❏ Choosing and evaluating a range of subject matter, symbols, and ideas
- ❏ Understanding the visual arts in relation to history and cultures
- ❏ Reflecting upon and assessing the characteristics and merits of their work and the work of others
- ❏ Making connections between visual arts and other disciplines

Multiple Intelligences and Learning Styles

- ☑ Visual/Spatial
- ❏ Logical/Mathematical
- ☑ Verbal/Linguistic
- ❏ Musical/Rhythmic
- ❏ Bodily/Kinesthetic
- ☑ Interpersonal/Social
- ❏ Intrapersonal/Introspective
- ❏ Naturalist

(Continued)

Opportunity for Assessment #5 (Continued)

Performance Task

Working in small groups, students are to create team mobiles representing various regions of the United States. Each team will present their mobile to the class as a group, also presenting information about their chosen region.

Assessment Technique

Portfolio Assessment—to show student progress over time; allows for extended product revision and development; ongoing feedback between students and teacher (see Figure 2.3).

ASSESSMENT DESIGN

A good performance assessment invents authentic problem situations that are rich in contextual detail. A context rich in detail supports students using multiple approaches, styles, strategies, and solutions, and good judgment. The assessment may be contrived, but it doesn't have to feel as if it is. It is realistic to the extent that it provides the feel of the challenge and motivates students to want to master it. The student will lose sight of the fact that he or she is doing this for a grade if the tasks presented are worth mastering.

The following guidelines can be used in the design of performance assessments.

1. Performance tasks should be authentic, meaningful, and worth mastering.

2. The set of tasks should be a valid sample from which broad and more abstract generalizations about the underlying principles can be made.

3. The evaluation criteria should be authentic, with points awarded or deducted for essential successes and errors.

4. The performance standards that anchor the evaluation should be genuine **benchmarks,** not arbitrary cut scores or provincial school norms.

5. The context of the problems should be rich, realistic, and meaningful to the students.

6. The task evaluation should be feasible and reliable.

7. The assessment results should be reported and used so that all those concerned with the data are satisfied.

Performance assessment, in the context of brain compatibility, represents the synthesis of knowledge, experience, and skill. Performance assessment

Geography Mobile Presentation Rubric

CRITERIA EVALUATED	NOVICE BEGINNING 1 NOT YET	BASIC DEVELOPING 2 YES BUT	PROFICIENT ACCOMPLISHED 3 YES	ADVANCED EXEMPLARY 4 YES PLUS	RS	DM	FS
Quality and accuracy of geographical content	Weak level of geographic understanding evident	Good knowledge of geographic information but some gaps apparent	Consistently strong knowledge of geographic information	Complete and comprehensive mastery of geographic information		8	
Demonstrations of Content Knowledge							
Ability to Connect Concepts and Ideas	Few connections between learning concepts and ideas demonstrated	Some connections between learning concepts and ideas demonstrated	Specific connections between learning concepts and ideas presented frequently demonstrated	Consistently clear and specific connections between learning concepts and ideas presented		8	
Demonstrations of Thought Organization							
Coherency and idea sequencing	Few ideas are sequenced or coherent	Some ideas are sequenced and coherent	Most idea sequencing is well planned and coherent	All idea sequencing is consistently well planned and coherent		2	
Clearly focused and well-supported ideas	Few ideas are focused or supported	Most ideas are focused and well supported	Ideas are consistently focused and well supported	Ideas are sophisticated, comprehensive, consistently focused, and well supported		3	
Organization	Writing is aimless and disorganized	Organization is rough but workable	Writing has a beginning, middle, and end	Compelling opening, informative middle, and satisfying conclusion		2	

Figure 2.3

(Continued)

Geography Mobile Presentation Rubric (Continued)

CRITERIA EVALUATED	NOVICE BEGINNING 1 NOT YET	BASIC DEVELOPING 2 YES BUT	PROFICIENT ACCOMPLISHED 3 YES	ADVANCED EXEMPLARY 4 YES PLUS	RS	DM	FS
Demonstrations of Effective Speaking							
Word Choice	Repetitive or incorrect word usage	Word choices are often dull or uninspired	Some sophisticated word choices, others are routine	Word choices are vivid and sophisticated yet natural		2	
Sentence Fluency	Numerous run-on sentences and sentence fragments make reading difficult	Sentences are often awkward with run-ons and/or fragments	Sentences are constructed correctly but do not flow smoothly	All sentences are clear, complete, and of varying lengths		2	
Conventions	Numerous errors make information difficult to understand	Sufficient errors to distract listener	Most language conventions correct	Impeccable grammar throughout		2	
Evidences of Critical\Thinking							
Clarity of Analysis of Thought	Vague, nonspecific thoughts that lack organization	Many of the ideas have been well analyzed	Clear and logical thought analysis employed	Sophisticated, clear, and precise thought analysis throughout		2	
				TOTAL GRADE			

RS (Raw Score) refers to the total of all initial points achieved.
DM (Difficulty Multiplier) refers to the degree of difficulty and therefore the weight of the scoring factor.
FS (Final Score) is achieved by multiplying the RS by the DM.

Figure 2.3

tasks require students to use everything they know to bring about a creative resolution to the problem presented. Such tasks, therefore,

- Are complex (the total plan or strategy is not easily seen)
- Yield multiple and often "messy" solutions (each with its own costs and benefits)
- Entail nuances in student judgment and interpretation
- Encompass the application of multiple criteria (which can, at times conflict with one another)
- Involve uncertainty (all information regarding the task may not be given)
- Require student self-regulation of the thinking process
- Involve the ability to find structure in apparent disorder
- Require effort and considerable mental work on the part of the student

To further evaluate the quality and value of a potential performance assessment, the activity or task that the student is to undertake should

1. Afford students more than a single solution or strategy

2. Require more of students than simply the reproduction of a skill or a recollection of facts

3. Promote student learning from performing the assessment

4. Allow teachers to ascertain the level of student knowledge created by student effort

To build a task and a means for evaluating a student's performance on that task, teachers must define the standards (both performance and content) by which the task is to be evaluated. Teachers must thoroughly detail how the task should be administered, how the task should be carried out, and what the expectations are; teachers also must provide exemplary samples of achievement so that everyone involved is clear on what "excellence" looks like. Before students begin the performance task, any interventions or guidance by facilitators must be done without compromising the validity and integrity of the task being assessed.

BEYOND THE ANSWER KEY

An evaluation should reflect what is most important about doing an effective job, not what is easiest to score. A growing number of teachers recognize the value of using rubrics as instructional tools. To implement a scoring system that is as authentic as the task being scored, teachers must look beyond the traditional answer key. Learning to use rubrics (benchmarks and checklists included) will help teachers judge student work fairly and communicate their expectations to both students and parents. Such methods of evaluation are clear and logical, rather than vague and mysterious like other, more traditional methods of scoring. Students and parents alike know before the start of the task what "excellent" or "good" looks like (see Rubric Template, Figure 2.4).

Rubric Template

Criteria Evaluated	Novice Beginning 1 NOT YET	Basic Developing 2 YES BUT	Proficient Accomplished 3 YES	Advanced Exemplary 4 YES PLUS
Quality or characteristic	Description of identifiable characteristics reflecting a beginning level of performance	Description at basic level	Description at proficient level	Description at advanced level
Quality or characteristic	Description of identifiable characteristics reflecting a beginning level of performance	Description at basic level	Description at proficient level	Description at advanced level
Quality or characteristic	Description of identifiable characteristics reflecting a beginning level of performance	Description at basic level	Description at proficient level	Description at advanced level

Figure 2.4

RUBRIC DESIGN

High standards are the focus for education today. Yet, to avoid the danger of viewing standards as merely content to be covered, it is best to focus on the content in terms of desired performances (taking care to make such performance tasks as authentic and reflective of real life as possible, while also connecting to standards). Such performances (or project work) require evaluation criteria and models of finished work at the outset in order to illustrate the different quality levels for the students. These performance assessments are typically open-ended and therefore provide opportunity for numerous and varied student solution processes. Because such student solutions have limited restrictions, they cannot be scored using a traditional answer key; instead, they require a method of evaluating based on explicitly defined performance criteria.

A rubric is a widely used evaluation tool consisting of criteria, a measurement scale (i.e., a 4-point scale), and descriptions of the characteristics for each score point. Rubrics that have been well designed communicate the important aspects or elements of quality in the product or performance and guide educators in the evaluation of student work. In general, rubrics benefit students. If students know and understand the criteria in advance, they have clear goals to guide their work.

While it is necessary to provide students with the rubric in advance, it is effective only if the students have a clear concept of what is meant by "quality work." Because students sometimes find rubric language vague and confusing, teachers must look to provide those students with models that exemplify the work at the various levels described in the rubric. Such examples help to translate abstract rubric terminology into real and understandable terms. Providing students with several models demonstrating variety in solution approaches helps them avoid the pitfall of single-solution thinking.

Creating the Rubric

A scoring rubric is one way of communicating clearly articulated standards before, during, and after a unit of study. The term *rubric* refers to an established set of criteria used for scoring or rating student work (journals, portfolios, performances, etc.). A rubric is fundamentally a matrix upon which teachers can convey answers to the following questions:

- What are the student performance goals?
- Exactly what does the student know based upon benchmarked standards?
- What constitutes evidence of student understanding?
- What does mastery of the task look like?
- What errors would justify lowering a score?

Figure 2.5 charts each of the evaluation techniques used throughout this book.

A scoring rubric describes the levels of performance a student might be expected to attain relative to a desired standard of achievement. These (performance) descriptions tell the evaluator specifically which characteristics or signs to look for in a student's work, and then how to place that work on a predetermined scale or continuum.

The rubric design methodology used throughout this manuscript is based on the use of clearly delineated standards and a difficulty multiplier (adapted from the Olympics scoring modality used in competitive events such as diving, commonly referred to as the "degree of difficulty"). This degree-of-difficulty factor, designated the difficulty multiplier (DM), allows the rubric designer to weigh certain of the evaluation criteria/qualities more than others.

Evaluation Tools	As Illustrated by
Group Presentation Rubric	Figure 4.1
Observation Rubric	Figure 2.3
Paragraph Assessment Rubric	Figure 2.4
Performance Assessment Rubric	Figures 5.5, 6.4
Portfolio Evaluation Rubric	Figures 1.3, 2.7, 3.1, 3.3, 4.4, 4.7, 5.2
Presentation Rubric	Figure 6.7
Scoring Rubric	Figure 1.6, 3.4, 3.7, 5.4
Student Self-Assessment Outline	Figures 1.4, 5.3, 6.1, 6.8
Two-Level Rubric	Figure 2.1

Figure 2.5

CREATING THE DESCRIPTOR LEVELS

Because the new performance assessment models such as observations, portfolios, and performance tasks are totally different from traditional multiple-choice or short-answer tests, they cannot be scored in the traditional manner. An alternative assessment methodology is needed to provide an objective basis for evaluation, one that will withstand concerns about the reliability of scores based on human judgment. In an effort to deal with these concerns, new scoring tools and methods are constantly being developed and improved to go along with the new assessments. To be valid, these new tools and methods must be based on clearly articulated standards. A scoring rubric is one way of communicating such standards before, during, and after a unit of study.

Rubrics provide an excellent means of communicating standards and goals because they have the advantage of offering both students and parents the opportunity to understand what learning is taking place in the classroom as well as the content standards included in that learning. By using rubrics at the beginning of a study unit students know from the start exactly what the teacher's expectations are for achievement. There are no surprises as to the level of those expectations, or how those expectations will be evaluated.

A well-designed rubric using evaluation criteria/qualities based on standards from professional organizations such as the National Council of Teachers of Mathematics (NCTM) or the National Council of Teachers of English (NCTE) will withstand criticisms of vagueness and subjectivity while at the same time allowing for individual learner differences.

Once the evaluation criteria have been selected, the rubric designer must then describe each of the four descriptor levels in clear and specific terms. An easy way to do this is to think of the four levels as the following:

Novice/Beginning—Not Yet

Basic/Developing—Yes But

Proficient/Accomplished—Yes

Advanced/Exemplary—Yes Plus

The activity in this chapter, Class Pet Diet Graph, contains a rubric for Accurate Data Recording.

The criteria to be evaluated are as follows:

- Level of comprehension
- Quality of data
- Accuracy of data
- Clarity of graph
- Accuracy of graph
- Level of completeness

Using the four descriptor levels, the Proficient column (YES) is where the teacher describes the goals for the project.

Class Pet Diet Graph

Criteria to Be Evaluated	Novice 1 NOT YET	Basic 2 YES BUT	Proficient 3 YES	Advanced 4 YES PLUS
Level of Comprehension			Graph illustrates solid understanding of material.	
Quality of Research			Research quality is competent and complete.	
Accuracy of Data			Data are accurate with no more than one error.	
Clarity of Graph			Graph is easy to read and understand.	
Accuracy of Graph			All components are constructed correctly.	
Level of Completeness			All components are included.	

Using the Proficient column as a guide, the teacher will then use the Advanced (YES PLUS) column for description of work that exceeds grade-level expectations.

Class Pet Diet Graph

Criteria to Be Evaluated	Novice 1 NOT YET	Basic 2 YES BUT	Proficient 3 YES	Advanced 4 YES PLUS
Level of Comprehension			Graph illustrates solid understanding of material.	Unique graph illustrates sophisticated comprehension, clearly above grade level.
Quality of Research			Research quality is competent and complete.	Research quality is rigorous and exemplary.
Accuracy of Data			Data are accurate with no more than one error.	Data are accurate in every aspect.
Clarity of Graph			Graph is easy to read and understand.	Graph is exceptionally clear, concise, and easy to follow.
Accuracy of Graph			All components are constructed correctly.	All axes, labels, and information are executed with clarity and total accuracy.
Level of Completeness			All components are included.	All required components are included as well as additional ones such as a graph key.

Using the Proficient column as a guide, the teacher will then use the Basic (YES BUT) column for description of work that represents lower expectations.

Class Pet Diet Graph

Criteria to Be Evaluated	Novice 1 NOT YET	Basic 2 YES BUT	Proficient 3 YES	Advanced 4 YES PLUS
Level of Comprehension		Graph illustrates a moderate level of understanding.	Graph illustrates solid understanding of material.	
Quality of Research		Research quality is superficial.	Research quality is competent and complete.	
Accuracy of Data		Accuracy of data is uneven with some inaccuracies evident.	Data are accurate with no more than one error.	
Clarity of Graph		Parts of graph are clear, but others are confusing.	Graph is easy to read and understand.	
Accuracy of Graph		Most components are correctly constructed, but some are not.	All components are constructed correctly.	
Level of Completeness		Most components are included, but one or two are missing.	All components are included.	

Using the Basic column as a guide, the teacher will then use the Novice (NOT YET) column for description of work that represents expectations falling below grade level.

Class Pet Diet Graph

Criteria to Be Evaluated	Novice 1 NOT YET	Basic 2 YES BUT	Proficient 3 YES	Advanced 4 YES PLUS
Level of Comprehension	Graph illustrates little or no understanding.	Graph illustrates a moderate level of understanding.		
Quality of Research	Poor research quality with many inconsistencies.	Research quality is superficial.		
Accuracy of Data	Graph is confusing and misleading.	Accuracy of data is uneven with some inaccuracies evident.		
Clarity of Graph	Confusing construction of components leads to erroneous conclusions.	Parts of graph are clear, but others are confusing.		
Accuracy of Graph	More than two components are missing.	Most components are correctly constructed, but some are not.		
Level of Completeness	Data are of poor quality and have at times been used incorrectly.	Most components are included, but one or two are missing.		

COMPUTING THE GRADE: MAKING QUALITATIVE ASSESSMENTS QUANTITATIVE

The DM allows the rubric designer to give certain of the evaluation criteria/ qualities more weight than others. By using a DM, a rubric can be scored in a manner that will result in a grade based on a scale of 0 to 100. Each criterion/ quality to be graded is assigned a numerical value of 4, 3, 2, or 1 (the raw score [RS]) depending on its level of distinction on the evaluation continuum. Multiplying the RS by the DM produces a final score (FS) for that particular criterion/quality. After each criterion has been evaluated in this manner, the resulting sum will be the total numerical grade.

While this score is not a percentage grade, it does create a grade range that is familiar to the student. In other words, if a student earns a 3 in every category (Proficient), the final score is 75, which in this situation translates to a grade of B. The following chart is to guide the evaluator in the scoring of such grades. Figure 2.6 illustrates how a score is computed, and Figure 2.7 shows how that score becomes a grade.

Raw Score	Difficulty Multiplier	Final Score
1–4	Column totals 25	RS x DM = FS
Sample Scoring		
3	4	12
4	6	24
2	10	20
3	5	15
	Column Total = 25	Final Score = 71
		71 = B (see Figure 2.7)

Figure 2.6

Grade Range

Raw Score	1		2		3		4	
	25		50		75		100	
	D		C		B		A	
	17–33		42–58		67–79		87–96	
	D–	D+	C–	C+	B–	B+	A–	A+
	13–16	34–37	38–41	59–62	63–66	80–83	84–87	97–100

Figure 2.7

Class Pet Diet Graph

Criteria to Be Evaluated	Novice 1 NOT YET	Basic 2 YES BUT	Proficient 3 YES	Advanced 4 YES PLUS	RS	DM	FS
Level of Comprehension	Graph illustrates little or no understanding.	Graph illustrates a moderate level of understanding.	Graph illustrates a solid understanding of material.	Unique graph illustrates sophisticated comprehension, clearly above grade level.		6	
Quality of Research	Poor research quality with many inconsistencies.	Research quality is superficial.	Research quality is competent and complete.	Research quality is rigorous and exemplary.		4	
Accuracy of Data	Graph is confusing and misleading.	Accuracy of data is inconsistent (some inaccuracies evident).	Data are accurate with no more than one error.	Data are highly accurate in all aspects.		5	
Clarity of Graph	Confusing construction of components leads to erroneous conclusions.	Parts of the graph are clear, but others are confusing.	Graph is easy to read and understand.	Graph is exceptionally clear, concise, and easy to follow.		3	
Accuracy of Graph	More than two components are missing.	Most components are correctly constructed, but some are not.	All components are constructed correctly.	All axes, labels, and information are executed with clarity and total accuracy.		4	
Level of Completeness	Data are of poor quality and have at times been used incorrectly.	Most components are included, but one or two are missing.	All components are included.	All required components are included as well as additional ones such as a graph key.		3	

RS (Raw Score) refers to the total of all initial points achieved.

DM (Difficulty Multiplier) refers to the degree of difficulty and therefore the weight of the scoring factor.

FS (Final Score) is achieved by multiplying the RS by the DM.

TOTAL GRADE   25

Graded Sample:

Class Pet Diet Graph

Criteria to Be Evaluated	Novice 1 NOT YET	Basic 2 YES BUT	Proficient 3 YES	Advanced 4 YES PLUS	RS	DM	FS
Level of Comprehension	Graph illustrates little or no understanding.	Graph illustrates a moderate level of understanding.	Graph illustrates solid understanding of material.	Unique graph illustrates sophisticated comprehension, clearly above grade level.	3	6	18
Quality of Research	Poor research quality with many inconsistencies.	Research quality is superficial.	Research quality is competent and complete.	Research quality is rigorous and exemplary.	3	4	12
Accuracy of Data	Graph is confusing and misleading.	Accuracy of data is inconsistent (some inaccuracies evident).	Data are accurate with no more than one error.	Data are highly accurate in all aspects.	3	5	15
Clarity of Graph	Confusing construction of components leads to erroneous conclusions.	Parts of graph are clear, but others are confusing.	Graph is easy to read and understand.	Graph is exceptionally clear, concise, and easy to follow.	3	3	9
Accuracy of Graph	More than two components are missing.	Most components are correctly constructed, but some are not.	All components are constructed correctly.	All axes, labels, and information are executed with clarity and total accuracy.	4	4	16
Level of Completeness	Data are of poor quality and have at times been used incorrectly.	Most components are included, but one or two are missing.	All components are included.	All required components are included as well as additional ones such as a graph key.	4	3	12

RS (Raw Score) refers to the total of all initial points achieved.

DM (Difficulty Multiplier) refers to the degree of difficulty and therefore the weight of the scoring factor.

FS (Final Score) is achieved by multiplying the RS by the DM.

TOTAL GRADE	82

To help articulate criteria at each of the four levels, the following list of Rubric Criteria Descriptors can be employed:

Rubric Criteria Descriptors

Novice 1 NOT YET	Basic 2 YES BUT	Proficient 3 YES	Advanced 4 YES PLUS
Simplistic	Superficial	Competent	Sophisticated
Unreflective	Simple	Satisfactory	Elegant
Uncritical	Developing	Plausible	Inventive
Beginning	Intermittent	Justified	Profound
Limited	Seldom	Verified	Perceptive
Weak	Lacking	Supported	Complex
Immature	Unclear	Reflective	Explicit
Clumsy	Somewhat	Aware	Powerful
Vague	Generic	Thoughtful	Incisive
Confusing	Uneven	Able	Precise
Dull		Developed	Nuanced
Routine		Accomplished	Novel
Incomplete		Critical	Masterful
Underdeveloped		Complete	Penetrating
Inaccurate		Accurate	Demanding
Irrelevant		Relevant	Intuitive
Ineffective		Effective	Revealing
		Clear	Exemplary
			Mature
			Concise
			Innovative
			Creative

CONSISTENT SCORING AND RELIABILITY

The use of human evaluators raises concerns about the reliability and consistency of scores based on the judgment of an individual. The expense and the time involved in scoring such authentic assessments have also caused concern. In an effort to deal with these issues, new scoring tools and methods are constantly being developed and improved to go along with new assessments.

Some school districts have worked out complex auditing schemes to ensure inter-rater reliability. Blind scoring, that is, evaluation of a performance task without direct contact with or knowledge of the person being evaluated, may also be used. A simple yet effective way to check consistency is to reevaluate a few papers from the top of the pile after a whole stack has been scored to guard against applying a sliding standard. Evaluators can score student work in one of two ways: holistically or analytically. Holistic scoring is an evaluation system based on the overall impression of a sample of student work viewed as a whole. This system produces a single number, typically based on a 0-to-4- or 0-to-6-point scale, and is used when a relatively quick yet consistent scoring method is needed.

Analytical scoring involves the awarding of separate scores for different qualities or traits of a student's work. This type of scoring, while much more time consuming than holistic scoring, provides more detailed information. Because analytic scoring can best pinpoint areas in need of improvement, it is often used for diagnostic purposes or curriculum and instructional program evaluation.

Students as Evaluators

One of the greatest differences between classrooms that use performance assessments and those that do not is the degree to which students engage in reflection and metacognition. Through the process of reflection, students become increasingly aware of themselves as learners. For many students, reflection is an entirely new skill requiring a great deal of specific instruction and support. The teacher's role is to foster reflection by helping students learn to identify the characteristics of high-quality work (what excellence looks like) and then recognize it in their own work as well as in the work of others. Reflection involves the description of methods and results, as well as assessments of new learning. With help in developing a vocabulary to discuss what they observe, students can become more sophisticated in their comments and reveal higher-level thinking and metacognition. Teachers can use the following words to construct **open-ended questions** that elicit student reflection.

Analyze	Compare	Contrast
Define	Demonstrate	Describe
Examine	Explain	Explore
Express	Illustrate	Investigate
List	Present	Prove

It is important to keep in mind that if students are not made to understand the use of rubrics and other assessment tools before they begin a performance assessment, much of the benefit of the actual experience will be lost or wasted.

CONTENT COUNTS

Care must be taken that content is not overlooked when emphasizing student performance. Students may be creating, but they may not be gaining understanding of content. Maintaining learning content is critical because learning is more than merely doing enjoyable project work. If too much emphasis is on doing fun things to the neglect of content, the substance of the learning will become ambiguous, vague, or even absent altogether.

It is part of an educator's job to stress with parents that the use of brain-compatible authentic assessment is not devaluing or reducing content, but rather, it is expanding it so that students are able to apply the knowledge they learn. The need to reassure parents reflects the challenge of gaining public support for performance assessments. Today's parents grew up in a norm-referenced system, and that remains their frame of reference. Parents need to be made aware that performance assessments complement traditional tests; they are not meant to replace them. Communicating the results of performance assessment to parents can sometimes pose a challenge for educators. Figure 2.8, the Parent Communication and Reflection Letter, can improve school-home communication by providing a way of initiating and establishing parental involvement. Research has shown that when parental involvement becomes part of the learning process, students have a higher success rate than when parents are not involved.

EDUCATIONAL INFERENCES

There are no real absolutes in assessment. The benefits of using brain-compatible, standards-based assessment tools for students, teachers, and parents are numerous. Learners are empowered to achieve success when they know what is expected of them before they begin the task. When students clearly understand what is expected, they can strive to meet or exceed expectations. Students develop enhanced cognitive or knowledge-based processes and metacognitive

Parent Communication and Reflection Letter

Dear Parent or Guardian,

Student self-assessment is a dynamic and positive learning tool. Its effectiveness lies in the fact that it helps students to:

- Develop responsibility for their own learning
- Become motivated for improvement
- Internalize criteria for success
- Learn to use assessment for growth
- Think reflectively

The performance assessment process used in this class requires both student and teacher input. The process uses observations and judgments to evaluate performance based on clearly defined criteria. We invite you to be part of this performance assessment process.

Please look over and read everything in your child's portfolio. Each piece is accompanied by his/her performance assessment. The portfolios also include reflections and self-evaluations.

When you have read the portfolio, please discuss the work with your child. The following questions can help guide you in the discussion.

Which piece(s) of work in the portfolio tells you the most about his/her critical thinking or problem-solving skills?

What does it tell you?

What do you see as the strengths in your child's thinking skills?

What do you think needs to be addressed in your child's growth and development?

Other comments, suggestions

Thank you so much for investing this time in your child's education!

Figure 2.8

practices, thinking about and mentally monitoring their learning, because the known criteria allow for the self-monitoring of work.

Graphing activities enhance both cognitive and metacognitive processes. They are most challenging and meaningful when students collect the data and construct their own meaning from those data. OPPORTUNITY FOR ASSESS-MENT #6: Class Pet Diet Graph (the rubric example used earlier in this chapter) is a chance for students to gain understanding through the application and use of real-world situations (real pets and their actual food and water intake). Students at all levels can use this activity to their advantage. Secondary students can formulate theories and predict future outcomes from the data they've collected. In addition, they can collect data about the weight of the animals relative to their food intake and then construct appropriate ratios. Or they can observe the effect different brands of pet food have on the animal's weight and digestion. Elementary students can record and graph single elements of intake (just food pellets). For example, they can create a pictograph in which each actual pellet affixed to the graph represents 10 pellets fed to the class rabbit.

OPPORTUNITY FOR ASSESSMENT #6

Class Pet Diet Graph

Level Middle

Content Standards

Science: National Science Education Standards (NSES)

CONTENT STANDARD A: SCIENCE AS INQUIRY

A1. Abilities necessary to do scientific inquiry:

- ❑ Design and conduct a scientific investigation.
- ❑ Use appropriate tools and techniques to gather, analyze, and interpret data.
- ❑ Develop descriptions, explanations, predictions, and models using evidence and explanations.
- ❑ Recognize and analyze alternative explanations and predictions.
- ❑ Communicate scientific procedures and explanations.
- ❑ Use mathematics in all aspects of scientific inquiry.

A2. Understanding about scientific inquiry:

- ❑ Different kinds of questions suggest different kinds of scientific investigations.
- ❑ Current scientific knowledge and understanding guide scientific investigations.
- ❑ Mathematics is important in all aspects of scientific inquiry.
- ❑ Technology used to gather data enhances accuracy and allows for analysis and quantification of results.

(Continued)

Opportunity for Assessment #6 (Continued)

❑ Scientific explanations emphasize evidence, logically consistent arguments, and scientific principles and theories.

❑ Science advances through legitimate skepticism, and investigations sometimes result in new ideas and phenomena.

Mathematics: NCTM

STANDARD 1: NUMBERS AND OPERATIONS

❑ Understand numbers, ways of representing numbers, relationships among numbers, and number systems.

❑ Understand the meaning of operations and how they relate to one another.

❑ Compute fluently and make reasonable estimates.

STANDARD 4: MEASUREMENT

❑ Understand attributes, units, and systems of measurement.

❑ Apply a variety of techniques, tools, and formulas for determining measurements.

STANDARD 5: DATA ANALYSIS AND PROBABILITY

❑ Select and use appropriate statistical methods to analyze data.

❑ Develop and evaluate inferences and predictions that are based on data.

Multiple Intelligences and Learning Styles

❑ Visual/Spatial
☑ Logical/Mathematical
❑ Verbal/Linguistic
❑ Musical/Rhythmic

❑ Bodily/Kinesthetic
❑ Interpersonal/Social
❑ Intrapersonal/Introspective
☑ Naturalist

Performance Task

In small groups, students will make and record observations about the food and water intake of classroom pets over an extended period of time. Students will then graph the data, make predictions as to the future health of pets, and be able to defend these predictions based on researched information.

Assessment Technique

Scoring Rubric (see rubric placed earlier in chapter).

Student Samples (see Figure 2.9)

Advanced

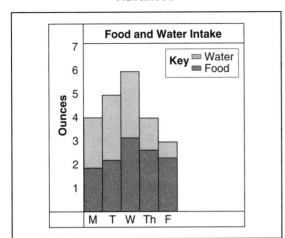

Proficient

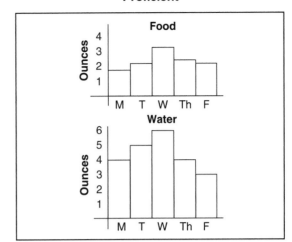

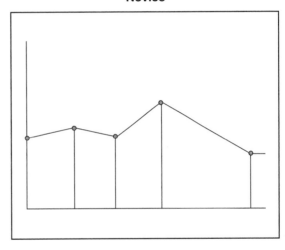

Basic

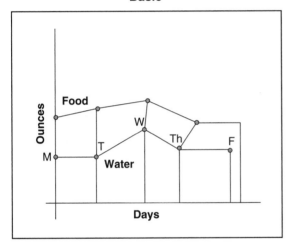

Novice

Figure 2.9

3

Multiple Intelligences and Brain-Compatible Assessment

It is of the utmost importance that we recognize and nurture all of the varied human intelligences, and all of the combinations of intelligences. We are all so different largely because we all have different combinations of intelligences. If we recognize this, I think we will have at least a better chance of dealing appropriately with the many problems that we face in the world.

—Howard Gardner (1987, p. 189)

LEARNING AND INTELLIGENCE

There is little agreement on a general definition of intelligence, but most persons would agree that it involves, at the least, the ability to learn and apply what has been learned. In addition, it is the ability to adapt to one's environment, or to modify that environment, or seek out and create new environments.

The concept of intelligence as something that could be quantified originated in France with the pioneering work of Alfred Binet and Theodore Simon. The two men published the Binet-Simon test of the mental ability of children in 1905, popularizing their theory that intelligence was tangible and could be objectively measured. Nearly two decades later, American Lewis Madison Terman coined the term *intelligence quotient (IQ)* and applied a normative scale to Binet and Simon's test. The resultant Stanford-Binet test has become one of the most widely used intelligence tests in the world. It is clear, however, that there is little correlation between IQ and what a person is able to learn and do in the real world. Many cognitive researchers are proving that intelligence is, in fact, an open, dynamic system, modifiable at any age and ability level.

MULTIPLE INTELLIGENCE THEORY

Almost 80 years after the first intelligence tests were developed, Harvard psychologist Howard Gardner challenged what had become commonly held beliefs about the nature of intelligence. In his book *Frames of Mind* (1983), he asserted that Binet and those that had built upon Binet's work had defined intelligence too narrowly, and that there exist many different kinds of intelligences. With his theory of multiple intelligences (MI theory), Gardner sought to broaden the prevailing view of human potential beyond the confines of the IQ score. He contended that intelligence had more to do with one's capacity for solving problems and creating products in a real-world setting than the IQ concept recognized.

Gardner provided a means of mapping the broad range of human abilities by grouping their capabilities into eight comprehensive categories or "intelligences," each considered equally important.

Visual/Spatial Intelligence is the ability to perceive the visual-spatial world accurately and to act upon those perceptions. This intelligence involves an awareness of color, line, shape, form, space, as well as the relationships that exist among these elements.

Logical/Mathematical Intelligence refers to acuity with numbers and the capacity to reason effectively. This intelligence includes the awareness of logical patterns and relationships, functions, and other related abstractions.

Verbal/Linguistic Intelligence is the capacity to use words effectively, whether orally or in writing. This intelligence includes the ability to handle syntax (language structure) as well as phonology (sounds) and semantics (meaning).

Musical/Rhythmic Intelligence is the capacity to perceive, discriminate, transform, and express musical forms. This intelligence includes sensitivity to rhythm, melody, and timbre of a musical piece.

Bodily/Kinesthetic Intelligence is the ability to use one's whole body to express ideas and feelings, and the facility to use one's hands to produce or transform things. This includes the physical skills of coordination, balance, dexterity, strength, flexibility, and speed.

Interpersonal/Social Intelligence is the ability to perceive and discern among the different intentions, motivations, and feelings of other people. This can involve sensitivity to facial expression, voice, and gesture, as well as the capacity for discriminating among an assortment of interpersonal cues, and the ability to respond effectively to those cues.

Intrapersonal/Introspective Intelligence is the capacity for self-awareness and self-knowledge as well as the ability to adapt oneself using that knowledge. This involves having an accurate and realistic image of oneself (strengths as well as limitations); an awareness of one's inner moods, intentions, motivations, temperaments, and desires; and the capacity for self-discipline, self-understanding, and self-esteem.

Naturalist Intelligence is the ability to make distinctions and form classes among objects (as in nature and the environment). The core of this kind of intelligence is the human ability to recognize plants, animals, and other parts of the natural environment. While this intelligence doubtless evolved as a means for humans to deal with their natural surroundings, it has been further evolved (or has been co-opted) to include the ability to distinguish between and recognize man-made objects such as cars, sneakers, and jewelry.

(Existential Intelligence, which refers to the human proclivity to ask fundamental questions such as "What is the meaning of life?" has been a candidate for several years, but Gardner has not yet included it on the list.)

Gardner contends that school systems tend to teach, test, reinforce, and reward verbal/linguistic and logical/mathematical abilities over the others. Recognizing the efficacy of each of the intelligences is central to brain-compatible instruction. It is logical then that persons having different intelligences enjoy and excel at different types of activities. Figure 3.1 outlines various activities associated with the different intelligences.

Using this chart as a resource for developing assessments that differentiate for a variety of combinations in students of these multiple intelligences, teachers can look to the column of relevant behaviors and design assessments that allow students to demonstrate their learning through these means. Any time students are given the opportunity to work on a project that interests them and that recognizes more than just verbal/linguistic and logical/mathematical intelligences, they will be better able to recall newly introduced information during related events in the real world.

The following OPPORTUNITY FOR ASSESSMENT allows students to demonstrate their understanding of the plot of a story by visually depicting the story line. Fairy Tale Storyboard is an elementary-level activity that can be easily adapted to other levels of classrooms. Middle- and secondary-level students can make a storyboard showing a lengthy story or novel. Students studying a foreign language can create their storyboards as evidence of understanding of a story or fairy tale in another language. The storyboard idea also works when studying many social studies topics because it shows a sequential progression of events.

Teaching to Gardner's Eight Intelligences: Ronis's Quick Reference Guide

Intelligence	Relevant Behaviors	Teaching Activities	Teaching Materials	Instructional Strategies
LINGUISTIC THE ABILITY TO USE LANGUAGE EFFECTIVELY	• Presenting persuasive arguments • Composing poetry • Recognizing subtle nuances in word meanings	Lectures, discussions, word games, storytelling, reading, journal or poetry writing	Books, tapes, records, computers and software	Read about it, talk about it, listen to it, write about it
LOGICAL/ MATHEMATICAL THE ABILITY TO FORM HYPOTHESES, DRAW CONCLUSIONS, AND REASON LOGICALLY	• Formulating and testing hypotheses • Quickly finding clear and direct solutions to problems • Generating mathematical proofs	Critical thinking tasks, brain teasers, problem solving, puzzles, number games, mental calculations	Calculators, computers, manipulatives, math games, puzzles	Think about it critically, analyze it, conceptualize it, quantify it
SPATIAL THE ABILITY TO OBSERVE DETAILS AS WELL AS IMAGINE AND "MANIPULATE" OBJECTS MENTALLY	• Creating mental images • Drawing an object accurately • Making fine discriminations among very similar objects	Visual presentations, artistic activities, creative games, visualizations	Graphs, maps, videos, construction toys (e.g., LEGO sets), art materials, optical illusions, cameras, picture library	See it, draw it, visualize it, construct it, color it, create it
BODILY/KINESTHETIC THE ABILITY TO USE ONE'S BODY SKILLFULLY	• Dancing • Playing a sport • Performing athletically	Dance, performance activities, sports activities, tactile activities	Building tools, art supplies, sports equipment, manipulatives	Build it, perform it, touch it, "feel" it inside, dance it
MUSICAL THE ABILITY TO CREATE, APPRECIATE, AND UNDERSTAND MUSIC	• Playing a musical instrument • Composing music • Identifying music's underlying structure	Lyrics, rhythms, and melodies that aid instruction	Musical instruments, tapes and tape recorder, CDs and CD player	Sing it, play it, "rap" it, listen to it, create it
INTERPERSONAL SENSITIVITY TO SUBTLE ASPECTS OF OTHER PEOPLE'S BEHAVIOR	• Demonstrating sensitivity to another's mood • Detecting another's underlying intentions and motives • Using knowledge of others to influence their thoughts and behaviors	Cooperative and collaborative learning, peer tutoring, peer counseling	Board games, room arrangement, role-play props	Teach it to each other, collaborate on it, interact with it
INTRAPERSONAL AWARENESS OF THE SUBTLE ASPECTS OF ONE'S OWN FEELINGS AND MOTIVES	• Discriminating among such similar emotions as anger and frustration • Recognizing the motives behind one's own behavior	Student reflection, independent study, alternative options for learning	Educational computer software, reflection guides, journals	Connect it to your personal life, analyze your behavior and motives
NATURALIST THE ABILITY TO RECOGNIZE PATTERNS IN NATURE AS WELL AS SUBTLE VARIANCES AMONG NATURAL OBJECTS AND LIFE FORMS	• Differentiating among similar species • Classifying natural forms • Practical application of one's knowledge of nature (e.g., gardening)	Moving the learning environment outdoors	Magnifying glass, drawing supplies, guidebooks	Through nature identify patterns and similarities, connect with previous experiences

Copyright © 2002 Diane Ronis, PhD

Figure 3.1

OPPORTUNITY FOR ASSESSMENT #7

Fairy Tale Storyboard

Level Elementary

Content Standards

Language Arts: National Council of Teachers of English/
International Reading Association (NCTE/IRA)

❑ Students adjust their use of spoken, written, and visual language (e.g., conventions, style, and vocabulary) to communicate effectively with a variety of audiences and for different purposes.
❑ Students employ a wide range of strategies as they write and use different writing process elements appropriately to communicate with different audiences for a variety of purposes.
❑ Students use spoken, written, and visual language to accomplish their own purposes (e.g., for learning, enjoyment, persuasion, and the exchange of information).

Visual Arts: National Art Education Association (NAEA)

❑ Understanding and applying media, techniques, and processes
❑ Choosing and evaluating a range of subject matter, symbols, and ideas
❑ Reflecting upon and assessing the characteristics and merits of their work and the work of others
❑ Making connections between visual arts and other disciplines

Multiple Intelligences and Learning Styles

☑ Visual/Spatial   ☑ Bodily/Kinesthetic
❑ Logical/Mathematical   ☑ Interpersonal/Social
☑ Verbal/Linguistic   ❑ Intrapersonal/Introspective
❑ Musical/Rhythmic   ❑ Naturalist

Performance Task

Working in small groups, students will create storyboards depicting the events of a fairy tale.

Assessment Technique

Portfolio Assessment—allows for extended product revision and development (see Figure 3.2).

MOTIVATION

Most learning style theories focus on the process used to initiate the learning. **Behaviorism** employs an extrinsic motivation system of rewards and punishments to cause learning to occur. MI theory, on the other hand,

Storyboard Rubric

CRITERIA EVALUATED	NOVICE BEGINNING 1 NOT YET	BASIC DEVELOPING 2 YES BUT	PROFICIENT ACCOMPLISHED 3 YES	ADVANCED EXEMPLARY 4 YES PLUS	RS	DM	FS
PORTFOLIO							
Depiction of Plot	Does not depict plot accurately or sequentially	Depicts most events accurately	Action is depicted accurately and sequentially	Depicts rising action, climax and falling action accurately and sequentially		7	
Clarity of Ideas	Vague and confusing	Some aspects are more easily understood than others	Easy to follow and understand	Precise, lucid, and extremely easy to follow		6	
Creativity	Renders events with little, if any, originality	Renders some events with originality	Renders events with originality and freshness	Renders all events in a highly unique, creative, and innovative manner		4	
Artistic Quality	Rendering shows uneven effort to achieve aesthetic result	Drawing is neat and demonstrates effort	Drawing is neat, colorful, and aesthetically appealing	Rendering displays much talent and skill		4	
Teamwork	Little evidence of constructive teamwork	Team members demonstrated intermittent cooperation	Group members worked constructively together	Group members demonstrated collaborative effort and synergy		4	
				TOTAL GRADE			

RS (Raw Score) refers to the total of all initial points achieved.

DM (Difficulty Multiplier) refers to the degree of difficulty and therefore the weight of the scoring factor.

FS (Final Score) is achieved by multiplying the RS by the DM.

Figure 3.2

is cognitive rather than behavioral because it works using innate and intrinsic motivation and is therefore brain compatible. By appealing to learners' various intelligences and strengths, MI theory makes the acquisition of new information more natural, positive, and more in line with the way the brain functions, thereby increasing student motivation.

The Cognitive Model

MI theory, unlike other current learning style theories, is a cognitive model in that it seeks to describe how individuals use their different intelligences to solve problems and create products. Unlike other models that are primarily process oriented, the MI approach is geared to how the human mind operates on the contents of the world (objects and people). The theory suggests that most people can develop all their intelligences to a relatively competent level of mastery. Whether or not these intelligences actually develop to their full potential depends on three factors: biological endowment (hereditary factors as well as traumas or injuries to the brain), personal life history (experiences with parents, teachers, peers, and others), and cultural and historical background (the time and place in which the individual was born and raised).

Consequences for brain compatibility: For strong development of all the intelligences, teachers must not allow any of them to be neglected. By recognizing multiple intelligences, teachers develop student strengths rather than accentuate student weaknesses.

The Personal Development Model

MI theory helps educators understand how their own personal learning style (their acute intelligences) affects their classroom teaching style. It is useful in helping teachers become cognizant of their own shortcomings and realize that every individual has the power to activate underdeveloped or paralyzed intelligences.

One of MI theory's greatest contributions to education is that, like brain-compatible learning and assessment, it presents the case for teachers to expand their repertoire of techniques, tools, and strategies beyond the traditional verbal and mathematical. For many educators who have done this instinctively, it corroborates and validates their natural and experiential understanding of how students learn. MI theory emphasizes the importance of an individual constructing his or her own understandings in a way that is personally meaningful. It was one of the initial theories that propelled the current attention in schools to the importance of differentiating instruction and assessment for students.

Consequences for brain compatibility: In a brain-compatible classroom, instruction and assessment utilize a multiple intelligences approach. The students are provided with a wide variety of topics, instructional methods, and presentation and assessment styles, which enable them to construct their own meaningful learning and encourage the evolution of sophisticated levels of understanding. To achieve greater comprehension, students need opportunities to discuss and debate unfamiliar concepts and ideas. They need to be able to test their understandings and participate in the higher cognitive levels of thinking that accompany such active dialogue. It is through such discussion and debate that shared meanings are developed and advanced. It is also the way in which meaningful learning becomes internalized and thus personalized. Without participatory dialogue, learning remains outside the person, removed from that person's experiences and mental connections. Where no personal connections are possible, learning continues to be elusive and difficult to retain.

The Alternative Educational Model

Many contemporary alternative educational models are essentially brain-compatible multiple-intelligence systems using different terminologies (and with varying levels of emphasis upon the different intelligences). Cooperative learning, for example, places its greatest emphasis on interpersonal intelligence; yet specific activities within the cooperative learning format can involve students in each of the other intelligences as well.

Consequences for brain compatibility: In the brain-compatible classroom, the teacher alternates between different methods of presentation, often combining different intelligences as well as providing numerous hands-on experiences and activities. The brain-compatible educator also encourages students to interact with each other in different ways (pairs, small groups, large groups). Because students have varying levels of ability in the different intelligences, any single teaching strategy could succeed with one group of students, yet not be as effective with another. Because each student's brain is unique, no single set of teaching strategies will work best for all students at all times. Because of these individual differences, the most effective teachers are those who are able to use a broad range of teaching strategies with their students.

BEYOND THE BLACKBOARD

Simply put, MI theory and brain-compatible instruction and assessment encompass all the methodologies that good teachers have always used in their teaching and evaluating. They reach beyond the textbook and blackboard to encourage student creativity, interest, and intelligence. Field-based research and MI theory provide a way for all teachers to reflect upon their best teaching methods and understand why these methods work. They also help teachers expand their current teaching style and assessment repertoire to include a broader range of methods, materials, and techniques for reaching an even wider and more diverse range of learners.

MI theory, by implication, calls for the implementation of brain-compatible learning and assessment for the following reasons:

- It provides variety and stimulation.
- The students create products using their own interests and skills.
- The pair learning model (or pair and share model, which harnesses the dynamic energy when two individuals interact) allows for individualized learning plans that are developed according to each student's learning style, assorted intelligences, strengths, interests, and needs.
- The teacher acts as a resource, facilitator, coach, and guide.

The OPPORTUNITY FOR ASSESSMENT #8 demonstrates how MI theory and brain-compatible learning work especially well together. Students are presented with an authentic and open-ended problem, are asked to work in cooperation with others, and can use their own interests and intelligences to resolve the problem. Invitation to Invention is a secondary activity that, like all of the tasks presented in this book, is easily adapted to other levels. Inviting elementary- and middle-grade students to create a life-improving invention can yield wonderful results. Younger students become acquainted with the process of scientific inquiry and many different ways to look at a problem. Teacher expectations at any level should be provided to students as they begin an activity so that they know in advance what "excellence" looks like.

MESSAGE CONFUSION

MI theory asks educators to use ordinary sources of information about how people around the world develop those skills important to their lives. It is not that standardized tests don't assess multiple intelligences; it is that they do so out of context. And it is precisely the learning and measuring of concepts in context that brings about the desired effect of students creating their own meaning in the context of their individual brain design.

MI theory challenges us to make changes in the assessment methods and techniques currently being used to evaluate learning. To have students learn via strategies grounded in MI and brain-compatible methodologies and then have them demonstrate their learning through narrowly focused standardized or unit tests is totally self-defeating. Many educational systems send an unintended but nevertheless dual message to students and the community that while learning through the use of the assorted intelligences is fun, novel, and exciting, when it comes down to what is really important, knowledge must be quantified and qualified in the traditional manner, by testing. If tests emphasizing the memorization of isolated bits and pieces of information are considered to be the only valid method of assessment, students and parents alike will be given the incorrect impression that knowledge has no connection with, or relevancy to, the real world outside the classroom.

OPPORTUNITY FOR ASSESSMENT #8

Invitation to Invention

Level Secondary

Content Standards

Science: National Science Education Standards (NSES)

Content Standard A:Science as inquiry

A1. Abilities necessary to do scientific inquiry:

- ❑ Identify questions that can be answered through scientific investigations.
- ❑ Design and conduct a scientific investigation.
- ❑ Use appropriate tools and techniques to gather, analyze, and interpret data.
- ❑ Develop descriptions, explanations, predictions, and models using evidence and explanations.
- ❑ Recognize and analyze alternative explanations and predictions.
- ❑ Communicate scientific procedures and explanations.
- ❑ Use mathematics in all aspects of scientific inquiry.

A2. Understanding about scientific inquiry:

- ❑ Different kinds of questions suggest different kinds of scientific investigations.
- ❑ Current scientific knowledge and understanding guide scientific investigations.
- ❑ Mathematics is important in all aspects of scientific inquiry.
- ❑ Technology used to gather data enhances accuracy and allows for analysis and quantification of results.
- ❑ Scientific explanations emphasize evidence, logically consistent arguments, and scientific principles and theories.
- ❑ Science advances through legitimate skepticism, and investigations sometimes result in new ideas and phenomena.

Technology: International Society for Technical Education (ISTE)

Basic Operations And Concepts

- ❑ Students demonstrate a sound understanding of the nature and operation of technology systems.
- ❑ Students are proficient in the use of technology.

Technology Productivity Tools

- ❑ Students use technology tools to enhance learning, increase productivity, and promote creativity.
- ❑ Students use productivity tools to collaborate in constructing technology-enhanced models, prepare publications, and produce other creative works.

Technology Communications Tools

- ❑ Students use telecommunications to collaborate, publish, and interact with peers, experts, and other audiences.
- ❑ Students use a variety of media and formats to communicate information and ideas effectively to multiple audiences.

Technology Research Tools

- ❑ Students use technology to locate, evaluate, and collect information from a variety of sources.
- ❑ Students use technology tools to process data and report results.
- ❑ Students evaluate and select new information resources and technological innovations based on the appropriateness for specific tasks.

Technology Problem-Solving and Decision-Making Tools

- ❑ Students use technology resources for solving problems and making informed decisions.
- ❑ Students employ technology in the development of strategies for solving problems in the real world.

Mathematics: National Council of Teachers of Mathematics (NCTM)

Standard 6: Problem Solving

- ❑ Build new mathematical knowledge through problem solving.
- ❑ Solve problems that arise in mathematics and in other contexts.
- ❑ Apply and adapt a wide variety of strategies to solve problems.
- ❑ Monitor and reflect on the process of mathematical problem solving.

Language Arts (Scientific and Reflective Writing): NCTE/IRA

- ❑ Students adjust their use of spoken, written, and visual language (e.g., conventions, style, and vocabulary) to communicate effectively with a variety of audiences and for different purposes.
- ❑ Students employ a wide range of strategies as they write and use different writing process elements appropriately to communicate with different audiences for a variety of purposes.
- ❑ Students conduct research on issues and interests by generating ideas and questions, and by posing problems. They gather, evaluate, and synthesize data from a variety of sources (e.g., print and nonprint texts, artifacts, and people) to communicate their discoveries in ways that suit their purpose and audience.
- ❑ Students use a variety of technological and information resources (e.g., libraries, databases, computer networks, and video) to gather and synthesize information and to create and communicate knowledge.

Multiple Intelligences and Learning Styles

- ☑ Visual/Spatial
- ☑ Logical/Mathematical
- ☑ Verbal/Linguistic
- ❑ Musical/Rhythmic
- ❑ Bodily/Kinesthetic
- ☑ Interpersonal/Social
- ❑ Intrapersonal/Introspective
- ❑ Naturalist

Performance Task

Students work in pairs using the **Internet** as a main research source to design and/or construct a machine, a process, or a theory that will improve an aspect of everyday life.

Assessment Technique (see Figure 3.3)

Scientific Method Rubric

CRITERIA EVALUATED	NOVICE BEGINNING 1 NOT YET	BASIC DEVELOPING 2 YES BUT	PROFICIENT ACCOMPLISHED 3 YES	ADVANCED EXEMPLARY 4 YES PLUS	RS	DM	FS
Question Quality	Few, if any, of the questions are valid, well stated, or tested	Some, but not all questions are valid and well stated; only a few are tested	Questions are valid, clearly stated, and tested	All questions are highly valid, precisely stated, and thoroughly tested		7	
Use of Inquiry/Discovery Method	Inquiry/discovery method rarely, if ever, used	Intermittent use of inquiry/discovery method	Inquiry/discovery method is used	Inquiry/discovery method is consistently and innovatively used		7	
Recorded Observations	Observations, recordings, inferences, and the synthesis of information are imprecise or specious	Observations, recordings, inferences, and the synthesis of information are inconsistently recorded	Observations, recordings, inferences, and the synthesis of information are competently recorded	Observations, recordings, inferences, and the synthesis of information are precisely recorded with total accuracy		6	
Technology	Technology used inappropriately	Some level of technological competence demonstrated	Competent use of technology	Technology used expertly, creatively, and as an integral part of the entire process		5	
				TOTAL GRADE			

RS (Raw Score) refers to the total of all initial points achieved.

DM (Difficulty Multiplier) refers to the degree of difficulty and therefore the weight of the scoring factor.

FS (Final Score) is achieved by multiplying the RS by the DM.

Figure 3.3

Brain-compatible MI instruction requires a fundamental restructuring in the way students demonstrate learning through an "authentic" system of assessments such as those described in Chapter 2. Authentic measures enable students to demonstrate what they've learned in context, in a setting that closely matches the environment in which they would be expected to use that learning in real life. Standardized instruments, on the other hand, almost always assess students in artificial settings, removed from any real-world context. These formal, externally developed assessments need to be balanced with authentic, brain-compatible assessments.

STUDENT STRENGTHS

The shift toward cognitive psychology and brain-compatible learning has educators increasingly interested in helping students develop and learn the use of thinking strategies. How students think has become as important as what they think about. Both brain-compatible and MI instruction and assessments provide the educational community with a language that speaks to the strengths and inner gifts of all students, not only those who happen to learn in either the verbal/linguistic or logical/mathematical mode.

A new curriculum model, one with a new emphasis, has been long overdue. The movement toward differentiated learning is a promising move toward formalizing this intent in schools. Such a curriculum design would be capable of speaking to all learners, each in their own particular brain language. Brain-compatible MI learning provides the tools to do just that.

Group work is one of the best ways for students to exercise their many intelligences. The team approach to problem solving emphasizes interpersonal intelligence, which is the main ingredient to success in the real world. OPPORTUNITY FOR ASSESSMENT #9 uses consumer economics to challenge students to use every member of the group and each of their intelligences to resolve an authentic problem. Auto Economics is a middle-level activity that can be tailored to suit other levels. Elementary students can investigate the price of candy (e.g., What is the price of the candy per piece bought in a bag? How many pieces can you buy with a dollar?). Secondary students can sell products of their own devising and track profit, loss, and cost to produce on computerized spreadsheet programs.

OPPORTUNITY FOR ASSESSMENT #9

Auto Economics

Level Middle

Content Standards

Mathematics: NCTM

Standard 1: Numbers and Operations

❑ Understand numbers, ways of representing numbers, relationships among numbers, and number systems.
❑ Understand the meaning of operations and how they relate to one another.
❑ Compute fluently and make reasonable estimates.

Standard 4: Measurement

❑ Understand attributes, units, and systems of measurement.
❑ Apply a variety of techniques, tools, and formulas for determining measurements.

Standard 6: Problem Solving

❑ Build new mathematical knowledge through problem solving.
❑ Solve problems that arise in mathematics and in other contexts.
❑ Apply and adapt a wide variety of strategies to solve problems.
❑ Monitor and reflect on the process of mathematical problem solving.

Standard 8: Communication

❑ Organize and consolidate mathematical thinking through communication.
❑ Communicate mathematical thinking coherently and clearly to peers, teachers, and others.
❑ Analyze and evaluate the mathematical thinking and strategies of others.
❑ Use the language of mathematics to express mathematical ideas precisely.

Social Studies: NCSS

Production, Distribution, and Consumption

Social studies programs should include experiences that provide for the study of how people organize for the production, distribution, and consumption of goods and services.

In schools, this theme typically appears in units and courses dealing with concepts, principles, and issues drawn from the discipline of economics.

Language Arts: NCTE/IRA

❑ Students read a wide range of print and nonprint texts to build an understanding of texts, of themselves, and of the cultures of the United States and the world; to acquire new information; to respond to the needs and demands of society and the workplace; and for personal fulfillment. Among these texts are fiction and nonfiction, classic and contemporary works.

❑ Students adjust their use of spoken, written, and visual language (e.g., conventions, style, and vocabulary) to communicate effectively with a variety of audiences and for different purposes.

❑ Students employ a wide range of strategies as they write and use different writing process elements appropriately to communicate with different audiences for a variety of purposes.

❑ Students conduct research on issues and interests by generating ideas and questions, and by posing problems. They gather, evaluate, and synthesize data from a variety of sources (e.g., print and nonprint texts, artifacts, and people) to communicate their discoveries in ways that suit their purpose and audience.

❑ Students use a variety of technological and information resources (e.g., libraries, databases, computer networks, and video) to gather and synthesize information and to create and communicate knowledge.

❑ Students use spoken, written, and visual language to accomplish their own purposes (e.g., for learning, enjoyment, persuasion, and the exchange of information).

Multiple Intelligences and Learning Styles

☑ Visual/Spatial   ❑ Bodily/Kinesthetic
☑ Logical/Mathematical   ☑ Interpersonal/Social
☑ Verbal/Linguistic   ❑ Intrapersonal/Introspective
❑ Musical/Rhythmic   ❑ Naturalist

Performance Task

Students, in groups of four, will compare and contrast new car data. Each team member will select his or her own auto for purchase based on data comparisons. Members will then research payment options, such as purchasing the car with a loan from a bank, using the dealership as a finance source, or leasing. Groups will make a presentation (e.g., written reports, graphs, charts) to the class comparing their different car and finance choices, as well as their conclusions.

Assessment Technique

Assessment to be accomplished via Performance Assessment consisting of informal observations by the teacher throughout the unit as well as a formal evaluation by teacher and peers using the Auto Economics Presentation Rubric (Figure 3.4).

Auto Economics Presentation Rubric

CRITERIA EVALUATED	NOVICE BEGINNING 1 NOT YET	BASIC DEVELOPING 2 YES BUT	PROFICIENT ACCOMPLISHED 3 YES	ADVANCED EXEMPLARY 4 YES PLUS	RS	DM	FS
ORGANIZATION							
Format	Confusing format (disorganized)	Uneven format and organization	Satisfactory format and organization	Unique and engaging format and logical organization		2	
Transitions	Abrupt transition from one idea to another, distracts audience	Transitions usually easy to follow, but one or two ideas may be unclear	Transitions usually easy to follow	All strong, smooth transitions (from idea to idea)		2	
Background Knowledge	Few team members demonstrate satisfactory background and topic knowledge	Several team members demonstrate satisfactory background and topic knowledge	All members demonstrate satisfactory background and topic knowledge	All members demonstrate exemplary and extensive knowledge of topic and background		6	
Visual Aids	Visual aids dull and hard to read or absent	Visual aids are attractive, but not always clear	Attractive, easy to understand, and follow	Highly attractive visual aids are original, engaging, easy to understand, and follow		4	
Introduction and Conclusion	Intro and conclusion are lackluster or incomplete	Either intro or conclusion is weak	Satisfactory intro and conclusion (closure)	Unique and creative intro and conclusion/closure		3	
Sensitivity to Audience Focus and Attention	Presentation style indifferent to audience focus	Presentation style remains the same throughout the presentation, whether or not the audience is focused	Adjusts presentation style to maintain audience focus and attention through most of the presentation	Continuously adjusts presentation style to maintain audience focus and attention throughout presentation		3	
Eye Contact	Little audience eye contact	Intermittent eye contact	Frequent audience eye contact	Continuous eye contact		2	
Speech Quality	Awkward, with incorrect grammar and word usage	Unsophisticated (poor vocabulary) but grammatically correct	Satisfactory use of vocabulary and grammatically correct	Sophisticated, professional and grammatically correct		3	
				TOTAL GRADE			

RS (Raw Score) refers to the total of all initial points achieved.

DM (Difficulty Multiplier) refers to the degree of difficulty and therefore the weight of the scoring factor.

FS (Final Score) is achieved by multiplying the RS by the DM.

Figure 3.4

4

Instruction and Assessment

I believe that today's high-stakes tests, as they are used in most settings, are doing serious harm to children. Because of unsound, high-stakes testing programs, many students are receiving educational experiences that are far less effective than they would have been if such programs had never been born.

—W. James Popham (2001, p. 1)

THE PULL OF THE NEWTONIAN PARADIGM

The term *paradigm* is used to describe the lens that orders, yet also limits, one's perception and thinking. A paradigm consists of all those deeply held beliefs and ideas that shape the collective grasp of reality—a compelling frame of reference that has a life of its own. The term *paradigm shift*, then, refers to the process whereby persons are able and willing to change their viewing lens. Changing one's frame of reference is an internal process initiated by the individual when the rules and theories about his or her world can no longer account for the information being perceived.

The dominant view of reality for the past several hundred years has been decidedly Newtonian. The industrial era was marked by a mechanistic worldview grounded in ideas espoused by Sir Isaac Newton during the late seventeenth century. One of the main aspects of the Newtonian paradigm was that almost everything in the world could be conceived of as machinelike. (Even the concept of solving a problem by "fixing it" is a mechanistic notion.) The goal of "fixing" human beings emerged as a corollary to Newton's theories and continues to influence ideas about instruction and education because it combines an explanation of reality with the supposed power to take charge of that reality. Under the mechanistic framework, problems are divided into distinct sections that are then "solved" in isolation. Behaviorism, a branch of psychology closely associated with education, is organized along such a framework and is characterized by the applications of rewards, deprivations, and/or punishments to control behavior mechanically. Gold stars, grades, training, detention, promotion, awards, incentive schemes, and penalties are the tools used to modify (fix) student behavior to conform (fit in) to society. The Newtonian paradigm served the world well during the industrial era, when factories were the social and organizational models for schools. Today, however, the traditional organizational underpinnings of schools are being eroded, in part because many of the larger systems that had formerly sustained education are now themselves changing or crumbling. The nuclear family, which replaced the extended family, is branching out and evolving into the single parent, divorced, and blended families. Community services and support have fallen on hard economic times while even the children are changing as a result of the influences of media and peer pressure.

Technological advances, scientific discoveries, and social change call into question traditional ways of thinking about schooling and the bureaucratic structure that supports it. Even in the face of profound upheaval, most persons cling to a traditional set of beliefs in which only experts create and evaluate knowledge and in which the teacher's job is to deliver and assess this knowledge, as well as decide where and when students should be graded on how much of the information they are able to store and recall on tests (Ronis, 2001). Such beliefs continue to permeate all aspects of education, including every decision (legislative or private), every meeting between teacher and parent, every budget deliberation, and every research study on teacher effectiveness. With the No Child Left Behind Act of 2001 (NCLB), however, we have seen the national government assume the mantle of ultimate arbiter of educational practice, in some instances tying what should be taught and how it should be taught to national funding for incorporation of teaching practices and content validated by specific forms of research evidence based on large experimental studies.

Ironically, the catalyst of the information explosion, the computer, has also made possible the brain imaging technology that has provided some fresh theories as to the way humans process information. Investigations into the **neurosciences** suggest that traditional and established methods of educating students actually inhibit rather than encourage their learning (Caine, Caine, McClintic, & Klimek, 2004). By discouraging, ignoring, or working against the natural learning processes of the brain, traditional didactic methodologies sometimes get in the way of learning and comprehension. Because the brain is intrinsically motivated by curiosity, it seeks out relevancy and connections. Passively receiving unconnected pieces of information through a lecture, or "telling," format does not always allow the brain to make the kinds of connections it seeks to make. Patterns give context to information that would otherwise be dismissed as meaningless. Active processing and internalization of information gleaned through experiential learning create the true path to understanding. Thus, it can be said that all meaningful learning is experiential.

Learning Climate Survey: Is the Environment in Your Classroom Conducive to Brain-Compatible Learning?

	Yes	No
1. Letter or number grades used for evaluation purposes		
2. Fragmented and compartmentalized curriculum		
3. Class organization by age and grade rather than student readiness		
4. Most learning outcomes specified as behavioral objectives		
5. Lack of attention to alternative answers or solution strategies		
6. Intelligence narrowly defined, emphasizing mainly language and mathematics		
7. General indifference toward individual learning styles		
8. Lack of group participation and/or poorly developed student groups		
9. General indifference to student interests or how those interests might relate to subject matter		
10. Indifference to the use of student experiences as sources for curriculum connections		
11. Motivation guided by external rewards and punishments (grades) rather than intrinsic ones (student satisfaction of accomplishment)		
12. Teacher delivery of information dominates class time		
13. Constant or intermittent interruptions (bells, announcements)		
14. Lack of teacher and/or team planning time		
15. External pressures to teach, test, and move on regardless of student comprehension or understanding		
16. Prescribed or mandated curriculum		

Figure 4.1

It follows then that grading, scoring, and ranking of individuals based on a stressful, one-time multiple-choice testing situation is antithetical to brain-compatible learning.

The Learning Climate Survey (Figure 4.1) has been created for teachers to assess the degree to which their classrooms are either supportive of, or actively interfering with, brain-compatible learning. Any "yes" responses point to a particular aspect of the learning environment that needs revision or reevaluation to make it more brain friendly.

It is becoming clear that the evolving role of the teacher is to facilitate the creation of meaningful knowledge and understanding. Curricula must be constructed as a scaffold upon which students stand and stretch to develop new abilities and meet new challenges. Instead of using traditional teacher-centered methods of instruction exclusively, a brain-compatible curriculum needs to be incorporated alongside the traditional one.

Renate Caine and Geoffrey Caine (1994, 1997a, 1997b; Caine et al., 2004) organized a learning framework from their vast research. When taken together, their brain-compatible learning principles (listed below) demonstrate how the brain functions as a system for learning.

1. The brain is a living system.
2. The brain is a social brain.
3. The search for meaning is innate.
4. The search for meaning occurs through patterning.
5. Emotions are critical to patterning.
6. Every brain simultaneously perceives and creates parts and wholes.
7. Learning involves both focused attention and peripheral perception.
8. Learning always involves conscious and unconscious processes.
9. We have at least two different types of memory.
10. Learning is developmental.
11. Complex learning is enhanced by challenge and inhibited by threat.
12. Each brain is uniquely organized.

The following Integrated Brain-Compatible Learning Principles for Assessment Purposes link certain of the 12 brain-compatible learning principles (previously listed) to those aspects of brain learning that specifically pertain to standards and assessment and are derived from my own work and experience. They concentrate on the aspects of brain research as it pertains to standards and assessment.

Principle 1: Every brain is uniquely organized, adaptive, and social.

Every person has the same set of systems but, due to genetics and/or different life experiences, each person develops into a unique individual. The differences can express themselves in terms of varied learning styles, talents, and intelligences. (See Chapter 3 for a discussion of multiple intelligence theory.)

Principle 2: Every brain is a device for both pattern seeking and meaning making.

Humans are innately motivated to search for meaning and relevancy. In general, the search for meaning refers to our making sense of all we experience. Although the ways in which individuals make sense of their experience change and evolve over time, the drive to do this always exists.

Principle 3: Every brain creates a personal perspective for meaning through connections created with the aid of the socialization process.

Verbal discourse creates individual sense making, which in turn, allows connections to be made between new information and previously assimilated knowledge. It is only through observation, discovery, conjecture, reflection, and group discourse that new knowledge can be processed, assimilated, and internalized, becoming a permanent part of the individual.

Principle 4: For every brain, the instinctive search for meaning occurs through patterning, with emotions being critical to that patterning.

The search for meaning occurs through patterning. The brain needs and automatically registers the familiar while simultaneously searching for and responding to novel stimuli. The brain attempts to discern and understand patterns as they occur and gives expression to unique and creative patterns of its own. For education to be effective, learners must be given an opportunity to formulate their own patterns of understanding.

Principle 5: For every brain, constructive challenge enhances learning while fear and threat hinder it.

The brain makes optimal connections when appropriately challenged in an environment that encourages risk taking. When placed in a threatening situation however, other "emergency" systems override the brain's innate inclination to make connections and satisfy curiosity.

Principle 6: For every brain, learning is developmental, involving conscious as well as unconscious processes that build upon what is already understood.

While the brain is being shaped and transformed throughout life, there are predetermined sequences of development in childhood that include periods of sensitivity for laying down foundations for later learning. (The capacity of young children to acquire a second language is much greater than that of an adolescent or adult, for instance.) If such periods are ignored or overlooked, the abilities atrophy and will eventually be lost altogether. The brain's propensity for information seeking, processing, and organizing suggests that to capitalize on such propensities, instruction and information must be organized in a manner that is brain compatible. Because emotion also is intrinsic to the education process, strategies for its inclusion cannot be neglected. Much of learning is unconscious—experienced as sensory input processed just below the level of awareness. Student comprehension may not occur immediately but rather after the brain has had some time to process the information. It follows then that teachers need to incorporate both reflective and metacognitive activities into lessons. Figure 4.2 is a list of the six brain-compatible learning principles just discussed.

Providing students with the guidelines for success before they undertake a task and the opportunity to work collaboratively with other students makes for the optimal emotional context for learning. The OPPORTUNITY FOR

Integrated Brain-Compatible
Learning Principles for Assessment Purposes

1. Every brain is uniquely organized, adaptive, and social.

2. Every brain is a device for both pattern seeking and meaning making.

3. Every brain creates a personal perspective for meaning through connections created with the aid of the socialization process.

4. For every brain, the instinctive search for meaning occurs through "patterning" with emotions being critical to that patterning.

5. For every brain, constructive challenge enhances learning while fear and frustration hinder it.

6. For every brain, learning is developmental, involving conscious as well as unconscious processes that build upon what is already understood.

Figure 4.2

ASSESSMENT #10, Stellated Dodecahedron, illustrates how assessment can be ongoing and integral to the learning process. The activity applies an open-ended problem (the challenge of creating original three-dimensional shapes) while at the same time "testing" the students' ability to accurately use a ruler and protractor. This activity is presented as appropriate to the middle school experience but can easily be adapted to an elementary activity by having students use manipulatives, such as blocks or felt pieces, to create new shapes. The performance task also can be adjusted to suit secondary students by adding a documentation component where students write about their processes in creating the shapes. (Such writing often allows the chance for student reflection and deeper understanding.)

OPPORTUNITY FOR ASSESSMENT #10

Stellated Dodecahedron

Level Middle

Content Standards

Mathematics: National Council of Teachers of Mathematics (NCTM)

Standard 3: Geometry

- ❑ Analyze characteristics and properties of two- and three-dimensional geometric shapes and develop arguments about relationships.
- ❑ Apply transformations and use symmetry to analyze mathematical situations.
- ❑ Use visualization, spatial reasoning, and geometric modeling to solve problems.

Standard 4: Measurement

- ❑ Understand attributes, units, and systems of measurement.
- ❑ Apply a variety of techniques, tools, and formulas for determining measurements.

Language Arts: National Council of Teachers of English/
International Reading Association (NCTE/IRA)

- ❑ Students adjust their use of spoken, written, and visual language (e.g., conventions, style, and vocabulary) to communicate effectively with a variety of audiences and for different purposes.
- ❑ Students conduct research on issues and interests by generating ideas and questions, and by posing problems. They gather, evaluate, and synthesize data from a variety of sources (e.g., print and nonprint texts, artifacts, and people) to communicate their discoveries in ways that suit their purpose and audience.
- ❑ Students use spoken, written, and visual language to accomplish their own purposes (e.g., for learning, enjoyment, persuasion, and the exchange of information).

Multiple Intelligences and Learning Styles

- ☑ Visual/Spatial
- ☑ Logical/Mathematical
- ☑ Verbal/Linguistic
- ❑ Musical/Rhythmic
- ❑ Bodily/Kinesthetic
- ☑ Interpersonal/Social
- ❑ Intrapersonal/Introspective
- ❑ Naturalist

Performance Task

Students learn methods for achieving accuracy with rulers and protractors. They then practice those skills by dividing a semicircle into five congruent, adjacent angles, each measuring 36 degrees. Once comfortable with the ruler and protractors, the students begin construction of the stellated dodecahedron model (a three-dimensional, twelve-pointed star). After completing the model, students are encouraged to create their own three-dimensional shapes using the acquired knowledge of geometry and their own imaginations.

Assessment Technique

Portfolio Assessment—allows for a picture of the processes and improvement over time and allows for student work samples. The Dodecahedron Rubric (Figure 4.3) helps to keep the assessment objective and allows students to understand the criteria upon which they will be evaluated.

Dodecahedron Portfolio Assessment Rubric

CRITERIA EVALUATED	NOVICE BEGINNING 1 NOT YET	BASIC DEVELOPING 2 YES BUT	PROFICIENT ACCOMPLISHED 3 YES	ADVANCED EXEMPLARY 4 YES PLUS	RS	DM	FS
CONSTRUCTION							
Measurements	Low level of accuracy (more than 6 errors)	Uneven level of accuracy (3-6 errors)	Linear and angular measurements are accurate (no more than 2 errors)	Total accuracy of all linear and angular measurements		5	
Shape/ Symmetry	Less than 3/4 of shape looks symmetrical	More than 3/4 of shape looks symmetrical	Good level of shape symmetry	Model constructed with perfect symmetry		5	
Model Integrity and Stability	Model can easily come apart	Model shape will change during handling	Model retains shape during handling	Stability and integrity of model will withstand abuse		5	
AESTHETICS							
Creativity	Plain surface used on model has become dirty due to sloppiness	Plain surface used on model; no adornment observed	Color and/or pattern used on surface of construction	Elegant and original surface textures/patterns used in construction		3	
Proportion	Product displays little or no aesthetic sense; proportions do not match at all	Some aspects of model overpower others	Proportions are visually pleasing	Aesthetically pleasing product; all proportions are in complete harmony		2	
STUDENT GROWTH							
Level of Progress	Little or no improvement exhibited	Slight improvement marks progress from one model to the next	Each new attempt marks improvement from previous one	Each attempt shows tremendous growth in skill and ability, resulting in task mastery		5	
				TOTAL GRADE			

RS (Raw Score) refers to the total of all initial points achieved.

DM (Difficulty Multiplier) refers to the degree of difficulty and therefore the weight of the scoring factor.

FS (Final Score) is achieved by multiplying the RS by the DM.

Figure 4.3

EMOTIONS IN CONTEXT

Traditionally, emotion and reason have been separated in the classroom. As a result, the day-to-day organization and management of schools may have been simplified, but sometimes at the expense of meaningful learning. Emotion and thought are connected at such a basic level that one cannot function without affecting the other. Emotions affect all learning: The stronger the emotion connected with an experience is, the more powerful the memory of that experience will be. When emotional input is added to the learning experience, the brain remembers the experience as being meaningful, and retention is increased. Emotion drives attention, which in turn drives learning and memory (Goleman, 1998, 2005). The more relevant a learning experience is, the more the learner becomes emotionally involved in that learning experience, making "meaningfulness" a prime motivator in the learning process.

In his book *A Celebration of Neurons* (1995), researcher Robert Sylwester suggests that the following are necessary both to maintain an optimal state of learning and for the future of meaningful and constructive education:

1. Accept and control emotions.

   Emotions simply exist. They are not learned in the same way facts are, nor can they be changed easily. However, how and when to use rational processes to override problem emotions and hold them in check can be learned. Educators must move toward the recognition and the inclusion of emotions in the classroom dynamic; they must encourage dialogue as well as accept and deal with the emotions that accompany the resolution of problems.

2. Use metacognitive activities.

   By focusing on metacognitive activities (those tasks that cause one to think about and reflect upon an experience) that encourage emotional verbalization and articulation, students will be more inclined to draw upon their own emotional references as a way of understanding the deeper motivation behind curricular goals.

3. Use activities that promote social interaction.

   School activities that provide emotional support tend to emphasize nonevaluative social interaction and engage the entire brain and body in the activity. Physical and arts education are curricular areas where social interaction can most easily be promoted. Unfortunately, although such subjects enhance learning, they are often treated as frills and are the first to be eliminated or curtailed when budgets get tight. (Most of the OPPORTUNITIES FOR ASSSESSMENT presented in this book involve cooperative group work.)

4. Use activities that provide emotional context.

   Memory has the ability to trigger emotion. The reoccurrence of the emotional state in which a memory was formed will trigger the recall of that memory. Emotion-laden classroom activities such as simulations, role playing, and cooperative group projects enable students to recall information during related events in the world outside the classroom. Anytime students are allowed to work and research a topic that interests them, they will be better able to recall that newly learned information when similar knowledge is needed in the future.

5. Avoid emotional stress.

An emotionally stressful learning environment reduces a student's ability to learn or process the information being taught. The use of ongoing authentic assessment as one evaluation modality helps to reduce the level of classroom stress. Although standardized tests compare and contrast different programs or student populations, they are ineffective at measuring student growth or educational quality (Popham, 2001). Alternative forms of assessment better gauge student abilities.

6. Recognize the relationship between emotions and health.

Emotion and health are closely related. Health education needs to address more than the healthy functioning of the body alone. The connection between a stimulating, emotionally positive classroom environment and the overall health of both students and staff must be included in the design of the curriculum.

THE NEED FOR STANDARDS

During times of transition, like those in which teachers find themselves today, the need to define and set goals is of great importance. Since NCLB was put into effect, a lot of heated debate has taken place regarding educational standards in the United States. While the need for standards is widely recognized, too often the standards being produced are lacking in measurable outcomes, contain vague language that refers to things that cannot be accurately assessed (such as love of literature), or are steeped in unrealistic expectations given available resources. Although most states have formulated standards for education, few states have assessments that match their standards. Instead, they find themselves forced to rely on the annual yearly progress of NCLB. This law, instead of edifying and enhancing assessment, restricts and limits evaluation to a statistical number resulting from a single high-stakes test.

The following list delineates characteristics that states and districts should include in their standards. Good standards must do the following:

- Be internationally benchmarked
- Describe a curriculum that can actually be taught
- Emphasize conceptual understanding and applications as well as basic knowledge and skills
- Incorporate examples of student work that meet the desired standards

To make standards compatible with brain-based learning, emphasis must be placed on inquiry and problem-solving methodologies over direct expository learning so that the brain's desire to organize information through pattern making can be engaged. A learner's natural curiosity and desire to make connections can provide the intrinsic motivation that propels "good" learning. Students enjoy new learning when they are able to do it and when they can see how it connects to their world.

Workplace skills will increasingly include critical thinking, problem solving, cooperation, and teamwork. Solving real-world problems enables students to create their own original and viable solutions and strategies. Developing a good set of standards is only the beginning of building a quality standards-based education system. Assessment and accountability are integral to a successful standards-based system. Implementing problem-solving instructional strategies requires the development of authentic systems of assessment that measure cognitive and manipulative skills rather than traditional assessments that measure memorization skills.

CONTENT STANDARDS AND PERFORMANCE STANDARDS

There are two distinct types of standards: content standards and performance standards. Content and process standards define the knowledge (the most important and enduring ideas, concepts, dilemmas, and information) and skills (the ways of thinking, working, communicating, reasoning, and investigating) essential to each discipline. Standards thus far produced by national association organizations, as well as by states, are in large part content standards. Content standards are difficult to use unless they are accompanied by performance standards. Performance standards specify "how good is good enough." They also indicate how competent a student demonstration must be to evidence attainment of the content standards. A performance standard has traditionally had three parts: the description, student samples, and commentaries. The description refers to what students must know and be able to do (the content standard). The samples of student work are to demonstrate the level and quality of work needed to meet that standard. And the commentaries on the student samples are needed to explain those features that raise the work to the particular standard level. The inclusion of student sample work is the key to making the standards usable by teachers, students, and parents. Any student should be able to look at a performance standard and say, "Now I understand what I need to do. I can learn to do that."

TEACHING METHODS AND INSTRUCTIONAL MATERIALS

Content is an essential ingredient for ensuring high-quality education for every student. However, content alone does not guarantee high-quality educational programs. Teacher methodology and style shape and influence what students learn. Because good teachers use different strategies at different times for different purposes, different and varied teaching techniques should also become part of the standards dialogue.

Good standards and assessments inevitably create a need for curriculum materials that are matched to those standards. The needed curriculum materials differ from what is most generally available. What educators need are materials grounded in content and based on brain-compatible instruction and assessment methodologies. Such materials would concentrate on only a few key concepts but would go into each of those concepts in depth. The materials would focus on enabling students to grasp underlying concepts. Texts would do a better job of helping students apply what they learn in the classroom to real-world, complex problems without sacrificing any of the strength of the core disciplines. The touchstone of such new curriculum materials would pay careful attention to the constant production of student work that meets the standards for that subject and grade level.

The OPPORTUNITY FOR ASSESSMENT #11, Cartoon Creation, is another example of how student achievement can be assessed in a brain-compatible manner. Because there is no set answer and the uniqueness of a student response is prized over a student's ability to guess what the teacher thinks is a "correct answer," the activity works with the brain not against it. The performance task offered here is geared to the secondary level but can be easily reframed to fit the standards for elementary- and middle-level students. Instead of analyzing, comparing, and contrasting economic systems (appropriate to the secondary level), elementary students can create cartoons depicting the various characteristics and types of human groups (families, villages, countries). Correspondingly, middle school students may construct cartoons that represent concepts such as Federalist and anti-Federalist positions during the debate on the ratification of the Constitution.

NO CHILD LEFT BEHIND

According to President George Bush, NCLB was designed to change the culture of America's schools by closing the achievement gap, offering more flexibility, giving parents more options, and teaching students based on what works.

Under the Act's accountability provisions, states were to describe how they would close the achievement gap and make sure all students, including those who were disadvantaged, achieve academic proficiency. They were to produce annual state and school district report cards that would inform parents and communities about state and school progress. Schools that did not make progress would be required to provide supplemental services, such as free tutoring or afterschool assistance; take corrective actions; and, if still not making adequate yearly progress after 5 years, make dramatic changes to the way the school is run.

According to the U.S. Department of Education's Web site, www.ed.gov, accountability is central to the success of NCLB: States are required to set high standards for improving academic achievement in order to improve the quality of education for all students. Under NCLB, each state would establish

(Continued on page 79)

OPPORTUNITY FOR ASSESSMENT #11

Cartoon Creation

Level Secondary

Content Standards

Social Studies: NCSS

Individuals, Groups, and Institutions

❏ Social studies programs should include experiences that provide for the study of interactions among individuals, groups, and institutions.

Production, Distribution, and Consumption

❏ Social studies programs should include experiences that provide for the study of how people organize for the production, distribution, and consumption of goods and services.

Language Arts: NCTE/IRA

❏ Students adjust their use of spoken, written, and visual language (e.g., conventions, style, and vocabulary) to communicate effectively with a variety of audiences and for different purposes.
❏ Students use spoken, written, and visual language to accomplish their own purposes (e.g., for learning, enjoyment, persuasion, and the exchange of information).

Visual Arts: NAEA

❏ Choosing and evaluating a range of subject matter, symbols, and ideas
❏ Understanding the visual arts in relation to history and cultures
❏ Reflecting upon and assessing the characteristics and merits of their work and the work of others
❏ Making connections between visual arts and other disciplines

Multiple Intelligences and Learning Styles

☑ Visual/Spatial
❏ Logical/Mathematical
☑ Verbal/Linguistic
❏ Musical/Rhythmic

❏ Bodily/Kinesthetic
☑ Interpersonal/Social
❏ Intrapersonal/Introspective
❏ Naturalist

Performance Task

Student pairs create a cartoon depicting one or more aspects of the relationship between the economic systems of capitalism and communism.

Assessment Technique

Student Self-Assessment Outline (see Figure 4.4)

Student Samples (see Figure 4.5)

Economic Systems Cartoon Student Self-Evaluation

Name _____ Date _____

How to Grade the Project

Were the economic concepts expressed clearly and accurately?

Was the cartoon well thought out, planned, and executed?

Was the cartoon neatly drawn?

How to Grade the Effort

Superior (E)

_____ My work was superior/excellent.

_____ I made many positive contributions to the effort in every way possible.

_____ I encouraged and assisted my partner when help was needed.

_____ I was key to our success.

Satisfactory (S)

_____ My work was complete and correct.

_____ I made several positive contributions to the effort.

_____ I encouraged and assisted my partner at least once.

_____ I helped my group succeed.

Unsatisfactory (U)

_____ I could have done better.

_____ I did not help or encourage my partner.

_____ I did not worry about the project.

_____ I kind of goofed off.

Explain the reasons for the grades you gave yourself below.

_____

_____

_____

_____

_____

_____

_____

_____

_____

_____

_____

_____

_____

_____

_____

Figure 4.4

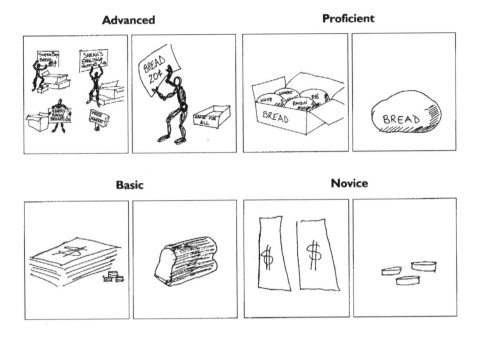

Figure 4.5

a definition of "adequate yearly progress" (AYP) to use each year to determine the achievement of each school district and school. The new definition of AYP is diagnostic in nature and intended to highlight where schools need improvement and should focus their resources. While the statute intended to give states and local educational agencies sufficient flexibility in how they direct resources and tailor interventions to the needs of individual schools identified for improvement, the results have been frustrating for all concerned. In other words, under NCLB, schools are held accountable for the achievement of all students, not just average student performance. The desire to ensure that schools are held accountable for all students meeting state standards represents the core of the bipartisan Act's goal of ensuring that no child is left behind. However, the result thus far falls short of the mark because such high-stakes measurements never do deal with children as individuals, but rather holds them all to an identical standard and to identical demonstrations, with the result that in many instances our new and cruel way of leaving children behind is to literally leave them behind by retaining them at grade level and then often not supplying the appropriate interventions to support their success and advancement (Mathis, 2003).

PROMISE FOR THE FUTURE

New suppositions are forging the way for very different views of delivering, receiving, and using information with the resultant implications for teaching, learning, assessment, and existing organizational models. The emerging new paradigm is grounded in a sense of connection, wholeness, and the need for creating experiences that link learning to new and deeper understandings (Caine et al., 2004). To assimilate the reality of an information-based society, educators must allow for a real change in the delivery of knowledge. Educators and others must be open to a basic paradigm shift in which meaningful knowledge and understanding are based on genuine insight and students are required to construct understandings for themselves. Meaningful knowledge and understanding are revealed through the application and use of such knowledge in real-world situations. In other words, it is the acquisition of meaningful knowledge rather than the memorization of information from so-called experts that defines a true act of learning.

Student survey and graphing tasks allow students to gather and synthesize information. OPPORTUNITY FOR ASSESSMENT #12, Television Time, provides students with the challenge of gathering data and constructing a visual representation of those data. There is no predetermined "correct" answer known only by the teacher, but instead the process of constructing meaning from data brings about a new and original result every time. While the processes may vary, the qualities (performance criteria) remain the same and are known before the work begins. The following performance task is suited to elementary students, but it can easily be modified to fit the needs and standards of middle school and high school students. Middle school teachers may want to include a larger sampling and require that averages (means and medians) be calculated. A presentation element could also be added. Building on the middle-level activities, secondary-level students might be asked to discuss and reflect upon the concept of survey reliability. Perhaps the upper-level students could "publish" their finding on the school's Web site, thereby allowing students an authentic audience for their authentic and original work.

OPPORTUNITY FOR ASSESSMENT #12

Television Time

Level Elementary

Content Standards

Mathematics: NCTM

Standard 1: Numbers and Operations

- ❑ Understand numbers, ways of representing numbers, relationships among numbers, and number systems.
- ❑ Understand the meaning of operations and how they relate to one another.
- ❑ Compute fluently and make reasonable estimates.

Standard 4: Measurement

- ❑ Understand attributes, units, and systems of measurement.
- ❑ Apply a variety of techniques, tools, and formulas for determining measurement.

Language Arts: NCTE

- ❑ Students adjust their use of spoken, written, and visual language (e.g., conventions, style, and vocabulary) to communicate effectively with a variety of audiences and for different purposes.
- ❑ Students use spoken, written, and visual language to accomplish their own purposes (e.g., for learning, enjoyment, persuasion, and the exchange of information).

Visual Arts: NAEA

- ❑ Using knowledge of structures and functions
- ❑ Choosing and evaluating a range of subject matter, symbols, and ideas
- ❑ Reflecting upon and assessing the characteristics and merits of their work and the work of others
- ❑ Making connections between visual arts and other disciplines

Multiple Intelligences and Learning Styles

- ☑ Visual/Spatial
- ☑ Logical/Mathematical
- ☑ Verbal/Linguistic
- ❑ Musical/Rhythmic
- ☑ Bodily/Kinesthetic
- ☑ Interpersonal/Social
- ☑ Intrapersonal/Introspective
- ❑ Naturalist

Performance Task

In pairs, students graph the results of a class survey. The graph is to represent the number of hours students spend doing their homework versus the number of hours they spend watching television.

Assessment Technique: Scoring Rubric (Figure 4.6)

Television Time Scoring Rubric

CRITERIA EVALUATED	NOVICE BEGINNING 1 NOT YET	BASIC DEVELOPING 2 YES BUT	PROFICIENT ACCOMPLISHED 3 YES	ADVANCED EXEMPLARY 4 YES PLUS	RS	DM	FS
Accuracy of Data	Numerous errors lead to poor accuracy level	Some accuracy, but several errors are clearly evident	Good accuracy with correct computation	Highly accurate, complex data with no errors		7	
Readability	Difficult to read and/or understand; confusing	Easy to follow in some places, but not throughout	Easy to follow and understand throughout	Extremely easy to understand at first glance; explicit		5	
Creativity of Graphic Design	Dull, simplistic layout and design	Predictable layout and design	Interesting layout and design	Elegant, innovative presentation		4	
Understanding of Graphic Representation of Data	Little or no demonstration of understanding	Comprehension evident in some places	Comprehension clearly evident throughout	Understands and synthesizes information throughout		7	
Neatness and Legibility	Messy and difficult to read	Legible in places but not throughout	Neat and easy to read	Immaculate, neat, and highly legible		2	
				TOTAL GRADE			

RS (Raw Score) refers to the total of all initial points achieved.

DM (Difficulty Multiplier) refers to the degree of difficulty and therefore the weight of the scoring factor.

FS (Final Score) is achieved by multiplying the RS by the DM.

Figure 4.6

Student Samples

Advanced

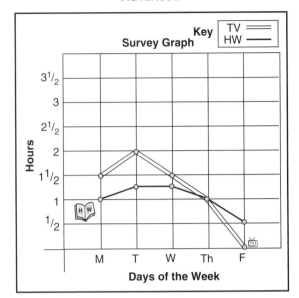

Proficient

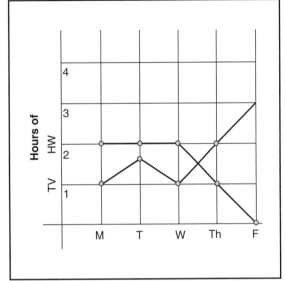

Basic

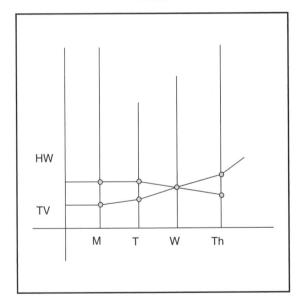

Novice

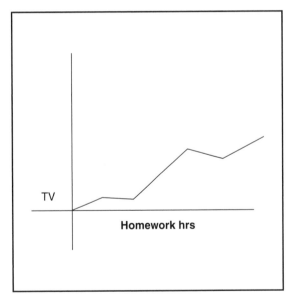

Figure 4.7

Wiring the Curriculum

Standards and Their Technological Applications

Technology helps teachers make interdisciplinary connections by providing access to worthwhile data. In addition, technology facilitates an in-depth explanation of . . . topics previously too complex for typical classrooms, especially when they involve real-world, messy data.

—Diane Ronis (2001, p. 19)

INTERACTIVE LEARNING

One of the best ways to encourage a transformation from the behaviorist reward/punishment mode to a more brain-compatible paradigm is through the use of technology. The technological world in which children grow up today is very different from the one in which today's adults grew up. Just about every child in the United States interacts daily with an assortment of technology and information media via telephone, television, video games, audio- and videotapes, DVDs (digital versatile discs), CDs (compact discs), or multimedia computer systems. At the same time, the workplace takes for granted a wide range of advanced and evolving technologies and complex, comprehensive information systems needed to streamline business operations.

STANDARDS, ACCOUNTABILITY, AND TECHNOLOGY

Over the years, social scientists and educational researchers have advocated the transformation of classrooms from passive to active environments. In order for today's young people to become competitive in tomorrow's marketplace, something more substantial than yesterday's pedagogical methodology is needed, particularly for those in high poverty or rural districts.

The President's Educational Technology Challenge, set forth in 1995, acknowledged that over 60% of America's newly created jobs in the twenty-first century would require technology skills (see http://www.ed.gov/PressReleases/10-1995/techno.html). The goal of the initiative was to ready young people for the demands of the technological workforce by mandating technological literacy. To this end, the following four pillars—challenges to the country's educators, parents, and business leaders—were established (U.S. Department of Education, 1998).

PILLAR I Modern computer and learning devices will be accessible to every student.

To make technology a viable educational tool, schools must have enough computers to provide full, easy access for all students, including students with disabilities. Full, easy access requires a ratio of at least five students to every one multimedia computer.

PILLAR II Classrooms will be connected to one another and the outside world.

Connections to local area networks (LANs) and the Internet turn computers into versatile and powerful learning tools. Access to these networks introduces students and teachers to people, places, and ideas from all over the world, ideas to which they might not otherwise be exposed.

PILLAR III Educational software will be an integral part of the curriculum and as engaging as the best video game.

Resources such as software, video, distance learning courses, and online resources hold promise to improve learning, increase the amount of time students spend learning, and engage students in problem solving, research, and data analysis, all of which help foster a brain-compatible learning environment.

Professional development is the key to effective technology integration as well as increased student learning. Teachers need access to technology and adequate time to acquire any and all skills necessary to integrate ever-evolving technology into their school's existing programs and activities.

Beyond the hype and rhetoric surrounding interactivity in education, students of all ages learn better when they are actively engaged in the learning process, whether that process comes in the form of a sophisticated multimedia package or a low-tech classroom debate on current events.

The urgent need for and emphasis on interactivity in the learning process is directly linked to the theory that each learner actively creates his or her own knowledge through direct and meaningful experience. In a school demonstrating interactivity, students communicate with other students through formal presentations, cooperative learning activities, and informal dialogue. Students and teachers communicate about their learning tasks in large groups, small groups, and one-to-one. Students have open access to and know about print and electronic information resources to inform their learning activities. They recognize the value of the information sources in their own communities and interact with community members to enhance their curricular studies with authentic information from primary sources.

The reason traditional expository teaching tends to turn students off is the lecture style of presentation, a format which cannot compete with the multimodal interactive formats of most other learning experiences that they encounter naturally in their environments outside the classroom. Field-based research shows that students need to be involved in the teaching/learning process to successfully expand their understanding of a given subject. The act of physically producing a physics experiment, while also exploring the social context in which the original experiment was performed, will hold more interest for students and have more educational value than listening to a lecture about how that same experiment was attempted centuries earlier. Learning becomes meaningful only after each learner has constructed his or her personal meaning from the experience itself.

By initiating their own learning, students are able to participate in productive questioning and probing for information that they can use immediately rather than waiting for the next question on a test or from a teacher. Information resources such as the Internet are central rather than peripheral to day-to-day learning activities. Through the use of brain-compatible problem-solving activities, students learn to gather their own data and then examine that information so that they can synthesize, analyze, and interpret the data in the context of the problems or questions they have identified.

Having students explore information through a variety of different instructional approaches often results in their becoming more interested and receptive to the subject they are studying. Because the brain is functioning with greater efficacy through these varied approaches, students are able to invest more of their mental energy in the learning and thereby commit concepts to memory with greater comprehension. Research shows that students who talk about how they and others think become better learners. When encouraged and given the opportunity and medium, students are willing to express opinions on almost any subject. By having the chance to articulate and share their thoughts, they are able to develop a more sophisticated understanding of a subject's meaning and relevance.

OPPORTUNITY FOR ASSESSMENT #13, Tessellation Transformation, offers a sophisticated performance task for secondary-level students that calls for the electronic manipulation of geometric shapes. The product serves as proof that the process was performed accurately. This task allows teachers to measure students' level of technological proficiency and their understanding of geometric concepts, all without putting pencil to paper. Middle-level students can gain understanding of geometric shapes by creating them on the computer using any number of software programs. Elementary-level students can learn to identify many-sided figures by using commercially available or teacher-constructed software programs.

OPPORTUNITY FOR ASSESSMENT #13

Tessellation Transformation

Level Secondary

Content Standards

Mathematics: National Council of Teachers of Mathematics (NCTM)

Standard 3: Geometry

- ❏ Analyze characteristics and properties of two- and three-dimensional geometric shapes and develop arguments about relationships.
- ❏ Apply transformations and use symmetry to analyze mathematical situations.
- ❏ Use visualization, spatial reasoning, and geometric modeling to solve problems.

Standard 8: Communication

- ❏ Organize and consolidate their mathematical thinking through communication.
- ❏ Communicate their mathematical thinking coherently and clearly to peers, teachers, and others.
- ❏ Analyze and evaluate the mathematical thinking and strategies of others.
- ❏ Use the language of mathematics to express mathematical ideas precisely.

Technology: International Society for Technology in Education (ISTE)

Basic Operations and Concepts

- ❏ Students demonstrate a sound understanding of the nature and operation of technology systems.
- ❏ Students are proficient in the use of technology.

Technology Productivity Tools

- ❏ Students use technology tools to enhance learning, increase productivity, and promote creativity.

Technology Communications Tools

- ❏ Students use a variety of media and formats to communicate information and ideas effectively to multiple audiences.

**Language Arts: National Council of Teachers of English/
International Reading Association (NCTE/IRA)**

- ❏ Students adjust their use of spoken, written, and visual language (e.g., conventions, style, and vocabulary) to communicate effectively with a variety of audiences and for different purposes.
- ❏ Students use spoken, written, and visual language to accomplish their own purposes (e.g., for learning, enjoyment, persuasion, and the exchange of information).

Visual Arts: National Art Education Association (NAEA)

- ❏ Understanding and applying media, techniques, and processes
- ❏ Using knowledge of structures and functions
- ❏ Reflecting upon and assessing the characteristics and merits of their work and the work of others
- ❏ Making connections between visual arts and other disciplines

Multiple Intelligences and Learning Styles

- ☑ Visual/Spatial
- ☑ Logical/Mathematical
- ☑ Verbal/Linguistic
- ❏ Musical/Rhythmic
- ❏ Bodily/Kinesthetic
- ☑ Interpersonal/Social
- ❏ Intrapersonal/Introspective
- ❏ Naturalist

Performance Task

Working in pairs, students create a series of tessellation designs from assorted basic geometric shapes. Students first experiment with single, unmodified shape tessellations and then go on to the intricacies of more sophisticated tessellation metamorphoses. The activity ends with a group competition for the most original and creative tessellation metamorphosis design.

Assessment Technique

Group Presentation Rubric (Figure 5.1)

Group Presentation Rubric for Use in Peer Evaluation

Part 1: Plan Content

Knowledge

_____ Strong knowledge of content and subject as demonstrated by quality of accuracy and detail

_____ Able to answer relevant, appropriate questions if asked

- Were all the objectives for this assignment carried out by the team (individual)?

_____ Does the unit topic have clear goals?

_____ Is there a unit rationale?

_____ Are the activities presented engaging?

_____ Does the presentation hold together?

_____ Are there clear unit objectives?

- How were these objectives carried out?

- Were visual aids provided? Were they helpful?

- How did or didn't they add to the presentation?

Organization

_____ Logical, sequential order to presentation

_____ Interesting beginning

_____ Informative middle

_____ Strong conclusion

_____ Well planned (not done "off the cuff")

_____ Interactive presentation (audience involvement)

Part 2: Presentation Skills

Superior Presentation (What excellent looks like)

_____ Excellent eye contact with entire audience

_____ Clear articulation (speaks clearly)

_____ Clearly audible (easily heard)

_____ Appropriate hand gestures and expressions

_____ Good supportive materials (charts, diagrams, posters)

_____ Demonstrates confidence

Comments:

Figure 5.1

Student Self-Evaluation

Excellent (E)

_____ The tessellation was unique, creative, well organized, easy to understand, and displayed interesting and creative insights

_____ The geometric shapes tessellated accurately, were easy to discern, and were carried beyond the basic requirements for this project

_____ Both team members were extremely well-prepared and contributed equally to the presentation discussion

_____ The coloring of the tessellation was sophisticated and contributed to the intricacy of the design

Satisfactory (S)

_____ The tessellation seemed adequate, but was not especially creative or unique

_____ Most of the shapes tessellated accurately

_____ Both team members contributed to the presentation discussion

_____ The coloring of the tessellation enhanced the design

Unsatisfactory (U)

_____ The tessellation appeared disorganized and was difficult to understand and/or follow

_____ The shapes did not tessellate accurately

_____ The presentation of the discussion was not done equally

_____ The tessellation was not colored, or the coloring detracted from the total design

In the space below, write several paragraphs to explain the reasons you gave the grade you did. Be sure to critique the presentation as well as the tessellation.

Figure 5.2

Student Work Samples

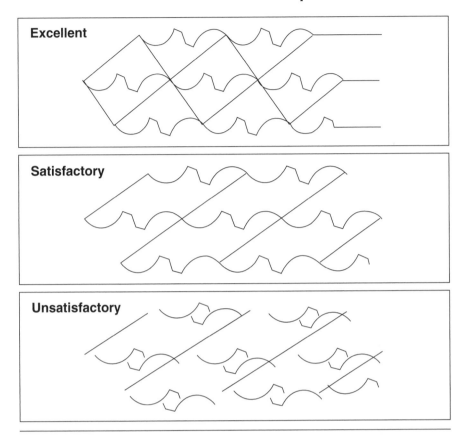

Figure 5.3

IN PERSPECTIVE

To be in step with interactive learning, teachers would do well to change their thinking so as to make the following shifts in outlook:

1. From linear to global view learning.

Traditional educational approaches were intended for the reading of printed material and textbooks, designed to begin at the beginning and continue straight through to the end. Today's children have evolved with a more global perspective, experiencing ideas that often come simultaneously from different vantage points.

2. From instruction to inquiry and discovery.

With new technologies, pedagogy has begun to shift from the traditional perspective to one in which learning partnerships and learning cultures are created and nurtured.

3. From teacher-centered to learner-centered education.

The focus of learning is now shifting from the transmitter (teacher) to the individual (learner), from a passive to a more active approach in which students discuss, debate, research, and collaborate.

4. From absorbing material to learning how to research, navigate, and learn.

Learners must go beyond knowledge analysis and move into the area of knowledge synthesis.

5. From school to lifelong learning.

Today knowledge is increasing at such an exponential rate that is difficult for anyone to keep pace with it all. It will become impossible for the citizens of the twenty-first century to learn all they will need for life while still in school. To cope with such a knowledge explosion, students must instead learn how to update and revise their knowledge base throughout their lifetime so as to keep pace with all the changes they will encounter.

6. From one-size-fits-all to individualized learning.

Today's technology allows students to have individualized learning experiences based on their backgrounds, individual talents, age levels, cognitive styles, and preferences.

7. From learning as torture to learning as fun.

When brain-compatible instructional methodologies are employed, a learner's innate curiosity can be linked to the wonder of discovery, transforming his or her perception of learning from one of work to one of pleasure.

8. From the teacher as transmitter (dispenser) to the teacher as facilitator (coach and guide).

With the teacher taking a back seat to the students in the students' construction of their own new knowledge, the teacher's role has been transformed from "sage on the stage" to one of "guide on the side."

TECHNOLOGY WITHOUT BORDERS

Many schools have yet to invest wholeheartedly in instructional technology, preferring instead to place computers in a single room where students use them once a week under a specialty teacher's supervision. In an effort to provide computer access to all students at an affordable cost, technology has come to be viewed in many schools and districts as a separate subject isolated from the rest of the curriculum in a "laboratory-style" arrangement. Such fragmented thinking is reminiscent of the Newtonian paradigm where knowledge is broken down into parts and then delivered in assembly-line fashion. For technology to be truly integrated, computers must take their rightful place in the classroom next to books, desks and chairs, and students, for in today's classrooms they are just as necessary.

Isolation and infrequent access have undermined the single most valuable aspect of the computer: its ability to cut across traditional subject boundaries as a practical and useful tool. Schools that treat technology as a separate, unrelated subject area called "computer literacy" have effectively minimized the potential impact computers can have on young people's learning.

The "laboratory" approach allows students to have access to only a small fraction of a computer in school. However, it is only with significant access that technology can have a major impact on educational practices or students' learning experiences. The fatal flaw in keeping computers separate from the everyday classroom environment is that any information learned about the computers today will be obsolete by tomorrow. It is only when computers are truly integrated into the curriculum (put into context) that students will gain the most valuable computer skill of all: the ability to use the computer as a natural tool for learning.

The OPPORTUNITY FOR ASSESSMENT #14, Multimedia Mapping, challenges elementary students to create a "map" (tutorial) that gives visual directions on how to use a DVD. The creation of maps, diagrams, and flow charts to depict operations (especially mathematical and technical ones) can be especially instructive for nonmathematical/logical thinkers because it actually creates a picture of the concept, helping those more inclined to visual/spatial learning. Further, writing about the process brings in verbal/linguistic learners and allows for self-reflection about the learning that has taken place during the performance of the task. Multimedia Mapping can be modified to suit other levels by keying in to content standards for those levels. Middle- and secondary-level students can diagram more complex operations like the creation of a spreadsheet. Advanced students might create a flow chart using presentation software showing the organization of a computer program of their own design.

SOFTWARE AND SERVERS AND SEARCH ENGINES, OH, MY!

Technology, specifically the computer, opens a world of opportunities for the classroom. However, technology, as with any other tool, is only as good as the way it is used. Even minimal technology training for teachers has a strong

(Continued on page 95)

OPPORTUNITY FOR ASSESSMENT #14

Multimedia Mapping

Level Elementary

Content Standards

Technology: ISTE

Basic Operations and Concepts

- ❑ Students demonstrate a sound understanding of the nature and operation of technology systems.
- ❑ Students are proficient in the use of technology.

Social, Ethical, and Human Issues

- ❑ Students practice responsible use of technology systems, information, and software.
- ❑ Students develop positive attitudes toward technology uses that support lifelong learning, collaboration, personal pursuits, and productivity.

Technology Productivity Tools

- ❑ Students use technology tools to enhance learning, increase productivity, and promote creativity.

Technology Communications Tools

- ❑ Students use a variety of media and formats to communicate information and ideas effectively to multiple audiences.

Technology Problem-Solving and Decision-Making Tools

- ❑ Students use technology resources for solving problems and making informed decisions.
- ❑ Students employ technology in the development of strategies for solving problems in the real world.

Mathematics: NCTM

Standard 3: Geometry

- ❑ Analyze characteristics and properties of two- and three-dimensional geometric shapes and develop arguments about relationships.
- ❑ Apply transformations and use symmetry to analyze mathematical situations.
- ❑ Use visualization, spatial reasoning, and geometric modeling to solve problems.

Standard 6: Problem Solving

- ❑ Build new mathematical knowledge through problem solving.
- ❑ Solve problems that arise in mathematics and in other contexts.
- ❑ Apply and adapt a wide variety of strategies to solve problems.
- ❑ Monitor and reflect on the process of mathematical problem solving.

Standard 8: Communication

- ❏ Organize and consolidate their mathematical thinking through communication.
- ❏ Communicate their mathematical thinking coherently and clearly to peers, teachers, and others.
- ❏ Analyze and evaluate the mathematical thinking and strategies of others.
- ❏ Use the language of mathematics to express mathematical ideas precisely.

Standard 9: Connections

- ❏ Recognize and use connections among mathematical ideas.
- ❏ Understand how mathematical ideas interconnect and build on one another to produce a coherent whole.
- ❏ Recognize and apply mathematics in contexts outside of mathematics.

Language Arts: NCTE/IRA

- ❏ Students adjust their use of spoken, written, and visual language (e.g., conventions, style, and vocabulary) to communicate effectively with a variety of audiences and for different purposes.
- ❏ Students use spoken, written, and visual language to accomplish their own purposes (e.g., for learning, enjoyment, persuasion, and the exchange of information).

Multiple Intelligences and Learning Styles

- ☑ Visual/Spatial
- ☑ Logical/Mathematical
- ☑ Verbal/Linguistic
- ❏ Musical/Rhythmic
- ❏ Bodily/Kinesthetic
- ☑ Interpersonal/Social
- ❏ Intrapersonal/Introspective
- ❏ Naturalist

Performance Task

In pairs, students will create a map (tutorial) showing the way to use a DVD. Every operation should be accounted for, from turning the machine on to quitting the program and putting it back where it belongs.

Assessment Technique

Scoring Rubric (see Figure 5.4)

---

impact on student achievement. Teachers with even a small amount of training are more likely to use computers in their classrooms more effectively than teachers who have no training at all. Teachers who have no training cannot afford to sit on the technological sidelines. Trepidation and lack of training, where computers are concerned, on the part of some teachers can be an opportunity to use a different and more brain-compatible pedagogy. Students should be encouraged to take the lead in making their own pathways to understanding the emerging technology. When the power of technology is placed in the hands of the students, they have more authentic learning experiences, construct their own meaning from their investigations, and gain confidence in

Multimedia Mapping Rubric

CRITERIA EVALUATED	NOVICE BEGINNING 1 NOT YET	BASIC DEVELOPING 2 YES BUT	PROFICIENT ACCOMPLISHED 3 YES	ADVANCED EXEMPLARY 4 YES PLUS	RS	DM	FS
Demonstration of Content Knowledge							
Ability to Connect Concepts and Ideas	Few connections between learning concepts and ideas demonstrated	Some connections between learning concepts and ideas demonstrated	Specific connections between learning concepts and ideas frequently demonstrated	Consistently clear and specific connections between learning concepts and ideas demonstrated throughout		5	
Demonstration of Thought Organization							
Clearly focused and well-supported ideas	Few ideas are focused or supported	Most ideas are focused and well supported	Ideas are consistently focused and well supported	Ideas are sophisticated, comprehensive, consistently focused, and well supported		6	
Organization	Writing is aimless and disorganized	Organization is rough but workable	Writing has a beginning, middle, and end	Compelling opening, informative middle, and satisfying conclusion		4	
Finished Product							
Quality of Sequencing	Missing steps or steps out of sequence lead to confusion	Some steps missing or out of sequence	Steps in sequential order	Highly detailed steps sequentially ordered		4	
Creativity and Innovation	Dull and routine presentation	Parts of presentation display innovation	Presentation displays innovation	Highly original presentation with audience-grabbing appeal		3	
Evidence of Critical Thinking							
Clarity of Analysis of Thought	Vague, nonspecific thoughts that lack organization	Many of the ideas have been well analyzed	Clear and logical thought analysis employed	Sophisticated, clear, and precise thought analysis throughout		3	
				TOTAL GRADE			

RS (Raw Score) refers to the total of all initial points achieved.

DM (Difficulty Multiplier) refers to the degree of difficulty and therefore the weight of the scoring factor.

FS (Final Score) is achieved by multiplying the RS by the DM.

Figure 5.4

their abilities to solve problems. Further, "having teachers and [students] learn and work together also models the community of learning and the community of leadership" exemplifying what cooperative, multiple-intelligence based, brain-compatible learning is all about (Maurer & Davidson, 1999, p. 459).

THE ROLE OF THE TEACHER

To develop self-initiated learners in the interactive, technology-oriented class-room, the teacher's role needs to evolve from one of fact-disseminator to the subtler role of coach and guide. In this continuously shifting role, teachers leave fact-finding to the computer and instead spend their time doing what they were meant to do: act as content experts through arousing curiosity, asking the right questions at the right time, and stimulating debate and serious discussion around engaging topics.

Instructor

When the computer is introduced into the classroom, an initial learning period occurs during which the young learners need time to become familiar and comfortable with the technology. It is during this period that the teacher needs to assume the most active role in instructing students, guiding them through new software and encouraging their exploration of the material. Always the teacher is the mediator of content and a resource for helping students evaluate content that they find and connect their independent learning to the standards.

Coach

As the students become more experienced with computers, the role of the teacher as technology tutor gradually changes to one in which the students are able to perform tasks independently, and peers begin to take over the role of instructor. The teacher then moves into the role of facilitator, providing guidance and support when needed and ensuring appropriate classroom behavior, while control of the situation passes more and more into the hands of the students.

Model

Students will be much more likely to use the computer as a practical, integrated tool for learning if they see the teacher doing the same. Using the computer during large and small group instruction and for recording stories and producing classroom signs and charts are ways in which the teacher can be a highly visible user of technology.

Critic

Responsibilities of the teacher in the computer-enriched classroom begin before the computer is introduced to the students. In providing a rich, challenging, and appropriate learning environment, teachers must take an active role in selecting the software that will truly enhance student learning and development.

World Wide Web Traveler

The Internet provides a rare opportunity for educators to engage in informal discussions on teaching strategies and a source of professional development. Traditionally, each classroom had been considered an island unto itself, with the teacher instructing, assessing, and remediating students independently from other teachers, even those within the same school. Networking now allows teachers to exchange lesson plans and advice as well as debate instructional methodologies with peers around the world with just a keystroke. Instead of having to wait for summer conferences on education reform, educators can now compare and contrast their work with relative ease and speed. In a sense, the Internet has electronically created a professional fraternity among educators.

SOFTWARE SELECTION

Despite changing and evolving classroom roles, it is still the responsibility of the teacher and the schools to select appropriate material for use in the classroom. Teachers must review and evaluate all the software before they expect students to use it. Rating systems such as those provided by the Entertainment Software Rating Board (ESRB) or the Recreational Software Advisory Council (RSAC) were developed by independent groups in conjunction with software publishers and can give educators a clue as to what a software title is all about. Labels on software and some Web sites alert consumers to the content and age appropriateness of material. They do not provide a quality or meaningfulness rating; that is up to the teacher or school's review committee to decide.

THE INTERNET

The easiest way for an educator to introduce the Internet into his or her classroom is by adding Internet components to already established lesson plans. While not all lesson plans allow themselves to be easily "Internetized," many others can be readily adapted. Making the Internet an everyday classroom activity, however, can be a two-edged sword. If undirected, students can become so engaged in using the Internet's extensive resources that too much time may be taken from other classroom activities. Therefore, it is best to start with a plan that first meets educational objectives and then modify that plan so that it will take advantage of online communication and navigational tools.

Lesson plans that best make the leap into cyberspace are those involving the following:

- Research on a particular topic
- Comparing and contrasting of information
- Information gathering from human sources such as other students or experts
- Critical thinking and analysis
- Researching and writing a report
- Use of graphics and art

- Collecting and analyzing data and building a database
- Conducting a survey through questionnaires
- Working in teams

After selecting those lesson plans that have the most potential, teachers can log onto the Internet and locate resource links that can be included in each lesson. The Internet Lesson Plan (Figure 5.5) is a way for teachers to outline their Internet project ideas.

Site Selection on the World Wide Web

What, exactly, are the criteria for valid information regarding a particular assignment? How are students to assess and evaluate when information is valid and reliable and when it isn't? Discussion of such issues and questions are a must for effective use of the Internet as a trusted research tool. The Internet provides access to information that is only a "click" away. While many Web sites frequently change their Internet address (or URL—Uniform Resource Locator) or cease to operate altogether, libraries, government agencies, and large corporations, for the most part, provide highly stable sites. Unfortunately, not all Web sites are of consistently high quality. The following guidelines can help in the selection of quality Web sites.

Desirable sites

- Have clearly identifiable sources, purpose, and content
- Are easily accessible in that the site loads quickly and displays accurate, regularly updated information
- Provide active hyperlinks to other sites to extend research capability
- Are free of any cultural, racial, religious, or gender bias

Student safety and privacy on the Internet should be of paramount concern to educators. Even though most schools have some type of censorware (a filtering program used to block access to some objectionable Web sites), teachers must monitor what sites students visit while at school because these programs are not always failsafe. One way to save time and to keep students away from offensive or inappropriate sites is to bookmark those sites that the teacher has previewed and deemed of value for the particular type of inquiry in which the students are engaged.

Exploring cyberspace can be very exciting for both teachers and their students. Surfing the surface of all of the topics found on the Internet does not promote critical thinking or provide the opportunity for the synthesis of that knowledge or time to reflect upon what has been seen. The OPPORTUNITY FOR ASSESSMENT #15 provides an ordered way for students to journal what they have found in the course of their travels, be critical about the resources sites they have explored, and provide time to meaningfully think about their experience. As presented here, Cyber Chronicles is a performance task for middle-level students, but it can be modified for use with secondary students as well. For secondary students, the performance standards (qualities evaluated) on the scoring rubric may be changed to reflect a higher level of expectation.

The Internet Lesson Plan

Lesson Title	Lesson Plan Type
Content Subjects and Grade Level	Description
Objectives (The students will be able to):	Educational Goals

Materials

Internet Resources Involved (Web sites):
URL:
URL:
URL:
URL:

Other Resources

Procedures and Timelines

Non-Internet Activities	Internet Activities

Problems and Issues That May Be Encountered

Solutions and Adjustments

Assessment Design

Follow-Up Activities and Extensions

Figure 5.5

(In addition, this task can be combined with any research assignment to enrich the research.) Elementary students may travel the information superhighway but with a bit more restraint and supervision. Teachers should bookmark sites that they have chosen for students to explore and chronicle.

OPPORTUNITY FOR ASSESSMENT #15

Cyber Chronicles

Level Middle

Content Standards

Language Arts: NCTE/IRA

- ❑ Students adjust their use of spoken, written, and visual language (e.g., conventions, style, and vocabulary) to communicate effectively with a variety of audiences and for different purposes.
- ❑ Students employ a wide range of strategies as they write and use different writing process elements appropriately to communicate with different audiences for a variety of purposes.
- ❑ Students apply knowledge of language structure, language conventions (e.g., spelling and punctuation), media techniques, figurative language, and genre to create, critique, and discuss print and nonprint texts.
- ❑ Students conduct research on issues and interests by generating ideas and questions, and by posing problems. They gather, evaluate, and synthesize data from a variety of sources (e.g., print and nonprint texts, artifacts, and people) to communicate their discoveries in ways that suit their purpose and audience.
- ❑ Students use a variety of technological and information resources (e.g., libraries, databases, computer networks, and video) to gather and synthesize information and to create and communicate knowledge.
- ❑ Students use spoken, written, and visual language to accomplish their own purposes (e.g., for learning, enjoyment, persuasion, and the exchange of information).

Technology: ISTE

Basic Operations and Concepts

- ❑ Students demonstrate a sound understanding of the nature and operation of technology systems.
- ❑ Students are proficient in the use of technology.

Social, Ethical, and Human Issues

- ❑ Students understand the ethical, cultural, and societal issues related to technology.
- ❑ Students practice responsible use of technology systems, information, and software.
- ❑ Students develop positive attitudes toward technology uses that support lifelong learning, collaboration, personal pursuits, and productivity.

(Continued)

Opportunity for Assessment #15 (Continued)

Technology Productivity Tools

❑ Students use technology tools to enhance learning, increase productivity, and promote creativity.
❑ Students use productivity tools to collaborate in constructing technology-enhanced models, prepare publications, and produce other creative works.

Technology Research Tools

❑ Students use technology to locate, evaluate, and collect information from a variety of sources.
❑ Students evaluate and select new information resources and technological innovations based on the appropriateness for specific tasks.

Multiple Intelligences and Learning Styles

☑ Visual/Spatial	❑ Bodily/Kinesthetic
❑ Logical/Mathematical	☑ Interpersonal/Social
☑ Verbal/Linguistic	❑ Intrapersonal/Introspective
❑ Musical/Rhythmic	❑ Naturalist

Performance Task

Students will work with teachers to select and pursue a research topic. While subject research is under way, students are to keep a journal of Internet sites they deem of value or interest.

Assessment Technique

Portfolio Evaluation using the evaluation rubric (Figure 5.6)

THE HUMAN TOUCH

Despite revolutionary advances in the field of educational computing, technology still remains simply a tool. Potentially powerful and stimulating, the computer is merely an inert object that could never be a substitute for the personal touch of the classroom teacher. However, the manner in which teachers implement technology and computer use in their classrooms ultimately will become the critical factor in education's future. By improving the connection between curriculum content, technology, and school process, classroom incorporation of technology will support each child's learning style or various intelligences in the best possible manner and will prepare students for future work environments in which technology is a seamless, ubiquitous presence.

Internet Journal Rubric

CRITERIA EVALUATED	NOVICE BEGINNING 1 NOT YET	BASIC DEVELOPING 2 YES BUT	PROFICIENT ACCOMPLISHED 3 YES	ADVANCED EXEMPLARY 4 YES PLUS	RS	DM	FS
Evidence of Critical Thinking							
Analysis and Judgment About Relevance of Web Site to Research Topic	Numerous poor choices demonstrate a lack of understanding of the research topic	Some site choices are relevant while others display little connection	Site choices are relevant to research topic	Site choices are highly relevant and specific with revealing topic connections		4	
Assessing Reliability of Site Information	None of the sites has been cross-checked to assess reliability	Only one or two of the sites have been cross-checked to assess reliability of information	Sites have been cross-checked with secondary sites to assess reliability of information	Sites have been cross-checked with multiple alternative sites to assess reliability of information		5	
Clarity of Analysis of Thought	Vague, nonspecific thoughts that lack organization	Many of the ideas have been well analyzed	Clear and logical thought analysis employed	Sophisticated, clear, and precise thought analysis throughout		4	
Entry Quality							
Entry Description	Weak descriptions lack substance	Uneven description quality	Solid description; easy to understand	Highly articulate, cogent, and concise		2	
Entry Detail	Low level of detail provided	Some entries show more detail than others	Attention to detail throughout	Highly sophisticated detail		2	
Entry Organization	Consistently weak organization	Some parts are better organized than others	Well organized	Erudite and complex organization		2	

Figure 5.6

(Continued)

103

Internet Journal Rubric (Continued)

CRITERIA EVALUATED	NOVICE BEGINNING 1 NOT YET	BASIC DEVELOPING 2 YES BUT	PROFICIENT ACCOMPLISHED 3 YES	ADVANCED EXEMPLARY 4 YES PLUS	RS	DM	FS
Journal Writing Quality							
Word Choice	Repetitive or incorrect word usage	Word choices are often dull or uninspired	Some sophisticated word choices, others are routine	Word choices are vivid and sophisticated yet natural		2	
Sentence Fluency	Numerous run-on sentences and sentence fragments make reading difficult	Sentences are often awkward with run-ons and/or fragments	Sentences are constructed correctly but do not flow smoothly	All sentences are clear, complete, and of varying length		2	
Conventions	Numerous errors make reading difficult	Sufficient errors to distract reader	Most conventions correct; only occasional errors	Impeccable grammar, punctuation, and spelling throughout		2	
				TOTAL GRADE			

RS (Raw Score) refers to the total of all initial points achieved.

DM (Difficulty Multiplier) refers to the degree of difficulty and therefore the weight of the scoring factor.

FS (Final Score) is achieved by multiplying the RS by the DM.

Figure 5.6

6

Collaborative Learning

The teacher is responsible for creating an intellectual environment where serious thinking is the norm. More than just the physical setting with desks, bulletin boards, and posters, the classroom environment communicates subtle messages about what is valued in learning . . . Are students' discussion and collaboration encouraged? If students are to learn to make conjectures, construct arguments and respond to others arguments, then creating an environment that fosters these kinds of activities is essential.

—National Council of
Teachers of Mathematics (2000, p. 18)

THE BENEFITS OF COOPERATION

One of the best instructional strategies for brain-compatible and multiple intelligence learning is the cooperative or collaborative model for learning. Cooperative or collaborative learning is a method of instruction whereby small groups of students of varying ability levels use a wide range of activities to acquire higher-order thinking skills. Dozens of major studies have concluded that the use of cooperative learning strategies can result in "positive student achievement, improved relations among different ethnic groups, and mainstreaming students with learning disabilities" among other benefits (Balkcom, 1992). In addition, cooperative learning is inexpensive when compared to other educational initiatives and easy to implement.

NEW UNDERSTANDINGS

Brain and field-based research and neuroscience have added to the collective understanding of how we learn, or don't learn, and why. Educators are beginning to gain more of a research-based understanding of the learning process, and from that understanding, they can make better decisions regarding how learning environments and instructional and assessment practices should be structured.

As a result of this greater understanding, it makes sense to follow the learning and assessment strategies recommended below to help promote a more brain-compatible style of teaching and assessing:

1. Provide variety and stimulation for students through the use of project units, field trips, speakers, and multimedia.

2. Have students actively create products, make presentations, or show exhibitions using their interests as a springboard for the project concepts.

3. Use the teacher as a facilitator, coach, arranger, expediter, or stage manager.

Neuroscientific as well as field-based research suggest new understandings and insights regarding teaching and learning, which appear to stress the following five factors:

- Students learn in a variety of different ways.
- Students do best when they actively participate in the learning.
- Students need to make connections not only intellectually but also physically and emotionally with the topics they are studying.
- Feedback between the student and the teacher helps to fine-tune the brain's patterns and programs.
- For maximum learning to occur, students must feel safe and secure.

The following OPPORTUNITY FOR ASSESSMENT allows for a performance assessment that includes student collaboration, discussion, and cooperation, as well as recognizes the need for students to formulate patterns of understanding by fitting them into the context of what they already know. It uses a familiar object (a kite) to bring about understanding of a new concept (two-dimensional geometric forms). Kites for Everyone! is an elementary-level activity but can be changed to accommodate learners at other levels. Middle-level students may be asked to construct a three-dimensional box-type kite, while secondary student projects may focus on the aerodynamic properties of their kites. The method of evaluation may be changed to best gain perspective on student growth and understanding.

OPPORTUNITY FOR ASSESSMENT #16

Kites for Everyone!

Level Elementary

Content Standards

Mathematics: National Council of Teachers of Mathematics (NCTM)

Standard 3: Geometry

- ❑ Analyze characteristics and properties of two- and three-dimensional geometric shapes.
- ❑ Use visualization, spatial reasoning, and geometric modeling to solve problems.

Standard 6: Problem Solving

- ❑ Build new mathematical knowledge through problem solving.
- ❑ Solve problems that arise in mathematics and in other contexts.

Standard 8: Communication

- ❑ Organize and consolidate their mathematical thinking through communication.
- ❑ Communicate their mathematical thinking coherently and clearly to peers, teachers, and others.

**Language Arts: National Council of Teachers of English/
International Reading Association (NCTE/IRA)**

- ❑ Students adjust their use of spoken, written, and visual language (e.g., conventions, style, and vocabulary) to communicate effectively with a variety of audiences and for different purposes.
- ❑ Students use spoken, written, and visual language to accomplish their own purposes (e.g., for learning, enjoyment, persuasion, and the exchange of information).

Visual Arts: National Art Education Association (NAEA)

- ❑ Understanding and applying media, techniques, and processes
- ❑ Reflecting upon and assessing the characteristics and merits of their work and the work of others
- ❑ Making connections between visual arts and other disciplines

Multiple Intelligences and Learning Styles

- ☑ Visual/Spatial
- ☑ Logical/Mathematical
- ☑ Verbal/Linguistic
- ❑ Musical/Rhythmic
- ☑ Bodily/Kinesthetic
- ☑ Interpersonal/Social
- ☑ Intrapersonal/Introspective
- ❑ Naturalist

(Continued)

Opportunity for Assessment #16 (Continued)

Performance Task

In pairs, students work together using pattern blocks and design templates to experiment with various possibilities for kite design. The students then write one sentence that describes the shapes they used in their kite design and their relative placement.

Assessment Technique

The Student Self-Assessment Outline (see Figure 6.1) helps in the development of self-directed learning skills.

THE SPECTRUM OF INTERDEPENDENCE

Cooperative learning fosters the development of independence in learners because it puts them, instead of their teacher, in charge of their own learning. The students are thus encouraged to gauge whether what they are doing is at the expected level of quality. The teacher, acting only as a guide, takes a back seat to the learners while they grow and become more self-sufficient, self-reliant, and competent in their expectations for themselves.

In other words, cooperative education fosters brain-compatible learning and assessment in the following ways:

1. Learners must feel safe and secure before any learning can occur. Therefore, it is incumbent upon the school to foster a feeling of security. Because complex learning is enhanced by challenge and inhibited by threat, the learning environment in the classroom must represent low stress and at the same time high challenge. (See Chapter 4, the section titled "Emotions in Context.")

2. The brain is social, allowing learning to thrive in group situations.

3. The search for meaning is innate; therefore, problem-solving situations allow the brain to make use of this innate search for meaning.

4. Because the brain searches for meaning through patterning and emotions are critical to patterning, the more a learner is emotionally and socially involved in his or her work, the more learning is retained for future application.

5. Group work favors brain-compatible learning because the brain simultaneously perceives and creates parts and wholes. In group work, a project can be dealt with as an entity while, at the same time, individual contributions that make up that entity are recognized.

KITES FOR EVERYONE!
Elementary Self-Assessment

1. Do all my geometric shapes fit together with no empty spaces?

2. Is my kite neat and original?

3. Does my math sentence tell something about my kite and the shapes inside?

4. Does my geometric shape design fill up the whole kite shape?

5. Can I make a kite shape-design and write a sentence about it by myself now?

Figure 6.1

The Competitive Classroom

Most competitive classroom situations are not conducive to learning for all students because each student must compete with his or her classmates to achieve a goal that only a few can attain. Such an environment feeds the perception that students are in a race against each other. Individual achievement is gained only at the expense of peers (Johnson & Johnson, 1987). Negative interdependence, mutual reliance that has become counterproductive and sometimes even destructive to the learning process, often results. Students try to secure an outcome that is beneficial to them while at the same time necessarily detrimental to those with whom they are competitively linked. A test graded on a curve breeds negative interdependence because a student who gets a very high score can "ruin the curve" for the rest of the group. By having more scores in the higher numbers, the normal curve is bumped up on the higher axis, making the passing grade higher, thereby causing more students to fail even though their test performance may not have been "bad." (See Chapter 1, Figure 1.2, Normal Distribution Curve.)

The Individually Structured Classroom

In the individually structured environment, students work by themselves to accomplish learning goals that are unrelated to the performance of other students. Goals are assigned, and student efforts are evaluated against a fixed set of standards with rewards given accordingly. Students work at their own pace, ignoring the other students in the class. In individualistic learning activities, students understand that their achievements are not related to what the other students do. In this modality, students will seek an outcome that is personally beneficial and will see the goal achievements of others as irrelevant. Special education classes are often designed for the individual. These students usually do not take the same standardized tests as the other students, and also do not have time limits when they are being tested. While such a learning environment might seem brain compatible on the surface, it does not afford students the benefit of either seeing what the other students are doing or, in any other constructive way, interacting with them. Because the students are more isolated (in daily classroom work and in testing situations), they will not be sufficiently prepared for real-world success.

The Cooperative Classroom

A cooperatively structured classroom involves students in ways that necessitate their working together for mutual goal accomplishment. Students in small groups are assigned information and/or materials for which all the group members are responsible. (They "sink or swim" together.) In a cooperative learning situation, there is a positive interdependence among the students. The learning goals can be reached only when and if all the group members succeed. The students, therefore, seek outcomes that are beneficial to all those with whom they are working. In order for this to occur, they need to discuss the information and/or material with each other, help one another understand it, and encourage each other to work hard. Their interaction creates interdependence, which is positive in nature.

According to David Johnson, Roger Johnson, and E. J. Holubec (1994), successful implementation of cooperative learning must involve five basic elements:

1. Positive interdependence

2. Face-to-face interaction

3. Individual accountability

4. Interpersonal and small group skills

5. Group processing

To achieve the first element of positive interdependence, mutual goals must first be established (goal interdependence). There must be a division of labor among the group members (task interdependence); division of materials, resources, or information among group members (resource interdependence); assignment of specific jobs or roles to each group member (role interdependence); and the giving of joint rewards (reward interdependence). The Cooperatively Structured Classroom (Figure 6.2) illustrates how interdependence is at the center of cooperative learning.

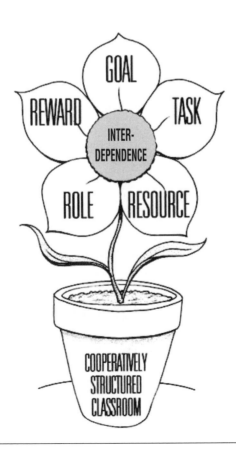

Figure 6.2

The second element, face-to-face interaction occurs when positive educational outcomes result from the positive interaction patterns and verbal exchanges taking place among students in carefully structured cooperative groups. Verbal summaries, giving and receiving explanations, and elaborations (relating the new learning to previous learning) are each important aspects of verbal exchange. In addition, verbal discourse helps to create individual sense making.

The third element, individual accountability, refers to the fact that cooperative learning groups will not succeed unless every member has learned the information and/or material, or has helped with and understands the assignment. For this reason, it is essential that the teachers frequently stress and assess individual progress so team members can support and help each other.

Because students rarely come to school with the social skills necessary for effective collaboration, instruction in the fourth element—interpersonal and small group skills—often falls to the teacher. It is up to the teacher to instruct the students in appropriate communication, leadership, trust, decision making, and conflict management skills as well as provide the motivation to use these skills to ensure effective group dynamics. Humans are not born instinctively knowing how to cooperate with others. Learning how to interact with others is just like learning other basic skills.

The fifth and final element for the successful implementation of cooperative learning is that of group processing. Processing is the concept of giving students the time and the procedural skills necessary to analyze how well their groups are functioning and how well they are utilizing the required social skills. Processing, when done correctly, provides accurate, nonthreatening feedback to the group regarding the procedures it is using to achieve the intended outcome. Feedback gives group members information that helps them improve performance while maintaining effective working relationships among members.

One way to energize group work is to infuse it with a performance component. The following OPPORTUNITY FOR ASSESSMENT is one that is particularly well suited to strengthening the group dynamic. Photosynthesis Rap presents students with the challenge of creating a song that will dramatize the process of photosynthesis. Students must possess an in-depth knowledge of the photosynthesis process before they can accurately and entertainingly present it to their classmates who will be evaluating the performance. The performance task can be modified to accommodate elementary classes by requiring only movement and not words or focusing on a content standard appropriate to that level. Secondary classes may be asked to portray more complex processes or give a series of performances. In any case, the task is authentic and provides for a real audience for the performance. Videotaping allows students to critique their own performance from a different perspective, and tapes can be made part of a group portfolio or can be shown at parents' night or to students in lower grades as instructional material.

OPPORTUNITY FOR ASSESSMENT #17

Photosynthesis Rap

Level Middle

Content Standards

Science (Life Science)

❑ Understands the cycling of matter and the flow of energy through the living environment

Music: National Association for Music Education
(formerly Music Educators' National Conference [MENC])

❑ Singing, alone and with others, a varied repertoire of music
❑ Improvising melodies, variations, and accompaniments
❑ Composing and arranging music within specified guidelines
❑ Evaluating music and music performances
❑ Understanding relationships between music, the other arts, and disciplines outside the arts

Language Arts

❑ Students adjust their use of spoken, written, and visual language (e.g., conventions, style, and vocabulary) to communicate effectively with a variety of audiences and for different purposes.
❑ Students use spoken, written, and visual language to accomplish their own purposes (e.g., for learning, enjoyment, persuasion, and the exchange of information).

Physical Education

❑ Demonstrates competency in many movement forms and proficiency in a few movement forms
❑ Applies movement concepts and principles to the learning and development of motor skills

Multiple Intelligences and Learning Styles

☑ Visual/Spatial
❑ Logical/Mathematical
☑ Verbal/Linguistic
☑ Musical/Rhythmic
☑ Bodily/Kinesthetic
☑ Interpersonal/Social
❑ Intrapersonal/Introspective
❑ Naturalist

Performance Task

In teams of four, students will create a rap song with accompanying movements that depicts the process of photosynthesis.

Assessment Technique

Performance Assessment—informal observation by the teacher as well as peer evaluation (see Figure 6.3)

Photosynthesis Rap Rubric

CRITERIA EVALUATED	NOVICE BEGINNING 1 NOT YET	BASIC DEVELOPING 2 YES BUT	PROFICIENT ACCOMPLISHED 3 YES	ADVANCED EXEMPLARY 4 YES PLUS	RS	DM	FS
Representation of Photosynthesis Process	Photosynthesis process presented inaccurately	Photosynthesis process presented with some degree of accuracy	Accurate representation of the photosynthesis process	Photosynthesis was represented clearly, accurately, and in an entertaining manner		7	
Quality of Lyrics	Lyrics made no sense scientifically	Lyrics made some scientific sense	Lyrics clearly made sense scientifically	Lyrics made sense from both musical and scientific standpoints		5	
Content Creativity	No originality or creativity displayed	Some creativity evident	Strong presentation of content	Rap was highly creative and original		3	
Movement, Music, Beat	Movement had no relation to the photosynthesis process	At times, movement suggested the photosynthesis process	Movement depicted photosynthesis process	Movement depicting photosynthesis was clever and imaginative		3	
Teamwork	Neither cooperation nor collaboration observable	Successful group dynamic visible in places	Successful team work observed	Group synergy and interaction clearly evident		3	
Eye Contact	Little audience eye contact	Intermittent eye contact	Frequent audience eye contact	Continuous eye contact		2	
Speech Quality and Articulation	Awkward, with incorrect grammar and word usage	Unsophisticated (poor vocabulary) but grammatically correct	Satisfactory use of vocabulary and grammatically correct	Sophisticated, professional, and grammatically correct		2	
				TOTAL GRADE			

RS (Raw Score) refers to the total of all initial points achieved.

DM (Difficulty Multiplier) refers to the degree of difficulty and therefore the weight of the scoring factor.

FS (Final Score) is achieved by multiplying the RS by the DM.

Figure 6.3

THE COOPERATIVE LEARNING ENVIRONMENT

Group investigations cooperative learning strategy is structured to emphasize critical and higher-order thinking skills. It can be modified to suit any grade level and does not require a curriculum overhaul to implement. It is highly brain compatible because the students actively construct their own learning through their own research. In this manner, each student's brain organizes the new information in its own way, a way that is meaningful to that individual. Most of the OPPORTUNITIES FOR ASSESSMENT presented in this book are group investigations.

Jigsaw II is another recognized cooperative learning format in which each member of a team is responsible for learning a specific part of a topic and then presenting their part to the rest of their group. This is not a good example of a brain-compatible learning format because the learning is fragmented and taken out of a natural context, making it very difficult for the brain to create any meaningful connections. STAD (Student Teams-Achievement Divisions) is a form of peer tutoring, where students of varying academic abilities form study groups composed of four or five members. The teams study the material initially presented by the teacher, and in this manner they are able to help each other learn. Although there is cooperation, there is no actual construction of knowledge by the individual team members themselves.

Educators with little background in cooperative learning sometimes believe they are using cooperative learning while in reality they are missing its essence. There is a critical difference between simply putting students into groups to learn and in structuring cooperative interdependence among students. Having students side by side at the same table talk with each other as they do their individual assignments is not cooperative learning, although such an activity does have a place in the classroom. Cooperative learning is not assigning a report to a group of students and letting one student do all the work with the others putting their names on the end product. Cooperative learning is the instructional use of small structured groups where students work together to maximize their individual learning and that of each member of the group.

The Teacher's Role

The teacher must develop an effective environment and pedagogy that are conducive to learning. Forming effective cooperative student groups, using lessons that require team problem solving, and developing methods to monitor both group work and individual learning are each the teacher's responsibility. In addition, it is the teacher who assigns the actual task to be completed cooperatively, determines what and how learning must be demonstrated by each individual student, and provides assistance to the group or individuals when needed. As facilitator and coach, the teacher also must monitor the functioning of the learning groups and teach those social skills necessary for successful learner collaboration.

Students' Roles

Collaborative learning encourages students to look to their peers rather than the teacher for assistance, feedback, reinforcement, and support. They are expected to share materials, interact, and encourage each other. In order to support individual student accountability, specific roles can be assigned to each member of the group. As students begin their group work, members learn how the roles function with the task at hand. Assigned roles create positive interdependence and teach students new skills. To support individual student accountability, it is beneficial to assign specific roles to each of the group members. Each group member should spend some time in each of the assigned roles. With experience, students will learn easily to shift from role to role.

Cooperative Group Activity Role Assignments

Group Coordinator

- Takes part in and contributes to the group activity
- Gets the group settled down and started on the activity
- Directs the activity and keeps all group members on task
- Encourages all members to contribute to discussions
- Helps group members to agree on answers to questions
- Reminds members to keep voices low during discussions

Group Recorder

- Takes part in and contributes to the group activity
- Keeps notes on all activities for group log entries (see Figure 6.4)
- Prepares a copy of the activity log sheet to be turned in to the teacher at the end of the class

Materials Person

- Takes part in and contributes to the group activity
- Picks up and distributes activity log sheets (see Figure 6.4)
- Picks up and distributes manipulatives and/or project supplies in an efficient manner
- Assumes responsibility for the care of manipulatives and/or project supplies
- Collects and turns in manipulatives and/or project supplies

Resource Person

- Takes part in and contributes to the group activity
- Finds additional resource materials when needed
- Decides when help is needed, and then asks the teacher for that help

In cooperative learning situations, students share materials, interact, and encourage each other. They explain the necessary information to one another and elaborate on the strategies and concepts they need to use. Exchanges between group members promote critical thinking, higher-level reasoning, and metacognitive thought. It's the act of explaining what one knows to one's groupmates and the development of essential listening skills that ultimately foster the understanding of how to apply knowledge and skills to new and different situations.

Assessing Group Learning

Because cooperative learning is group learning, group assessment must also be part of the equation. If the basic elements of cooperative learning are at work, group assessment means forming evaluations based on individual responsibilities performed toward some group end. All group members must be held responsible for their own learning as well as the learning of others, understand the concepts and assignments, demonstrate mastery of the assigned work, provide leadership, and assess the progress of the group. To assess the group and its members fairly, develop a rubric for the group as a whole as well as each individual member.

CONSCIOUS ATTENTION

Managing new approaches to teaching and learning requires a deeper understanding of how the brain works as well as an understanding of what motivates and engages people. Evidence suggests that the brain's ability to stay consciously attentive for extended periods of time is not only rare but also extremely difficult to achieve. The normal human brain cycles, with periods of highly focused attention followed by periods of less conscious attention. The brain requires these lower levels of conscious attention to process the learning it has accumulated during the highly focused period. If too much information is given without allowing enough processing time, the brain cannot perform well and optimal learning will not occur.

Brain-compatible cooperative learning supports the "processing time" concept because the time students discuss, write, work on projects, or peer-teach is the time when they are best able to process their learning. In addition, processing allows for student reflection. The ability to reflect upon learning takes **cognition** a step further, to a level commonly referred to as metacognition. Metacognition, or thinking about one's thinking (the ability to self-reflect), is a higher-order cognitive skill.

In order to help students learn to use their metacognitive skills, they must first be instructed in methods of self-reflection. The processes of helping students begin to be self-reflective means guiding the structure of their reflections. Figure 6.5 offers a way to structure student reflections.

Cooperative Group Activity Log

Group Members:

_____

_____

Class Section: _____ Group Name: _____

Project:

_____

_____

_____

_____

_____

Date	Name	Work Completed

Figure 6.4

Sample Questions to
Guide Students in Reflective Writing

Understanding the Problem Situation

❑ Can you tell me about this problem in your own words?

❑ Is anything missing, or has any unnecessary information been given?

❑ What, if any, assumptions are you making about the problem?

Planning the Strategy

❑ Can you explain your strategy to me?

❑ What have you tried so far?

❑ How did you organize your information?

❑ Is there a simpler problem related to this one that you might solve first?

Executing the Strategy

❑ Can you show me how you checked your work?

❑ Why did you organize your data this way?

❑ Why did you draw this diagram?

❑ How do you know whether what you are doing is correct? Logical?

Reviewing the Work

❑ Are you sure your strategy/solution is correct? Why?

❑ Could you have solved this problem differently?

❑ What made you decide to use this particular strategy?

Problem-Solving Communication

❑ Can you reword this problem using simpler terms?

❑ Can you explain what you are doing?

❑ How would you explain what you are doing to a teammate who is confused?

❑ Can you design your own problem using this same strategy?

Problem-Solving Connections

❑ Have you ever solved a similar problem? How is it the same? How is this different?

Self-Assessment

❑ Is this kind of problem solving easy or difficult for you?

❑ What makes this type of problem solving easy? What makes it difficult?

❑ In general, what kind of problem situations are especially hard for you? Which are easy? Why?

Figure 6.5

Metacognition and self-reflection are means of assessment, while observation is an important means of assessment integration. With observation, the teacher is able to monitor the learning as it occurs within the group. Performance tasks usually have an audience—in this case the teacher and the rest of the class. By learning what society values, students will be better equipped to self-evaluate.

Activities such as the one presented in OPPORTUNITY FOR ASSESSMENT #18 have been proven to foster positive interdependence, promote class morale, and improve student attendance. The Checks and Balances Video is a cooperative learning opportunity that, at the same time, recognizes individual strengths and intelligences. In the process of producing the video, students will necessarily become intimately familiar with the concept of check and balances or any other subject or concept the teacher assigns. The assessment task is presented here as appropriate to the secondary level, but just about any level (with varying degrees of coaching from the teacher) can learn from creating a video. Elementary students could act out a story or interact as phonemes to create words (or numbers to create math sentences). Middle-level students can create videos that dramatize a story or play of their own creation or television commercials designed to persuade students to buy the concepts of democracy or the free market system.

OPPORTUNITY FOR ASSESSMENT #18

Checks and Balances Video

Level Secondary

Content Standards

Social Studies: National Council for the Social Studies (NCSS)

Power, Authority, and Governance

❑ Social studies programs should include experiences that provide for the study of how people create and change structures of power, authority, and governance.

Language Arts: NCTE/IRA

❑ Students adjust their use of spoken, written, and visual language (e.g., conventions, style, and vocabulary) to communicate effectively with a variety of audiences and for different purposes.
❑ Students employ a wide range of strategies as they write and use different writing process elements appropriately to communicate with different audiences for a variety of purposes.
❑ Students conduct research on issues and interests by generating ideas and questions, and by posing problems. They gather, evaluate, and synthesize data from a variety of sources

(e.g., print and nonprint texts, artifacts, and people) to communicate their discoveries in ways that suit their purpose and audience.

❑ Students use spoken, written, and visual language to accomplish their own purposes (e.g., for learning, enjoyment, persuasion, and the exchange of information).

Technology: International Society for Technology in Education (ISTE)

Technology Productivity Tools

❑ Students use technology tools to enhance learning, increase productivity, and promote creativity.

❑ Students use productivity tools to collaborate in constructing technology-enhanced models, prepare publications, and produce other creative works.

Technology Communications Tools

❑ Students use telecommunications to collaborate, publish, and interact with peers, experts, and other audiences.

❑ Students use a variety of media and formats to communicate information and ideas effectively to multiple audiences.

Technology Research Tools

❑ Students use technology to locate, evaluate, and collect information from a variety of sources.

❑ Students use technology tools to process data and report results.

❑ Students evaluate and select new information resources and technological innovations based on the appropriateness for specific tasks.

Multiple Intelligences and Learning Styles

☑ Visual/Spatial   ❑ Bodily/Kinesthetic
❑ Logical/Mathematical   ☑ Interpersonal/Social
☑ Verbal/Linguistic   ☑ Intrapersonal/Introspective
❑ Musical/Rhythmic   ❑ Naturalist

Performance Task

Students will work together in groups of three or four, creating a videotape depicting the system of checks and balances in the U.S. government. Students are encouraged to use the Internet as a project research resource.

Assessment Technique

Presentation rubric to be completed by the teacher and the audience/class (see Figure 6.6) and self-assessment to be completed by individual team members about their own work (see Figure 6.7).

Presentation Rubric for Checks and Balances Video

Part 1: Video Content

Qualities Evaluated

❑ System of checks and balances was presented accurately

❑ Video clearly represented the major characteristics of a shared power system

❑ Extensive research was evident in the finished product

❑ Content of video displayed creativity and originality

❑ Presentation was well articulated and easy to understand

❑ Team functioned synergistically

Were all the objectives for this assignment carried out by the team?

Does the video have a clear goal/purpose?

Is there a rationale to the video?

Is the video engaging and entertaining?

How was the video's goal carried out?

Were visual aids provided? Were they helpful?

How did or didn't the visual aids add to the presentation?

Part 2: Video Organization

❑ Logical, sequential order to presentation

❑ Interesting beginning

❑ Informative middle

❑ Strong conclusion

❑ Well planned (not "off the cuff")

Comments:

Figure 6.6

Self-Assessment Evaluation
Qualities for Checks and Balances Video

How to Grade the Project

Were the required concepts expressed clearly and accurately?

Would a viewer understand the major characteristics of a shared powers system after viewing this video?

Was the video well thought out, planned, and executed?

Was the video informative? Entertaining?

How to Grade the Effort

SUPERIOR: (E)

_____ My work was superior/excellent.

_____ I made many positive contributions to the effort in every way possible.

_____ I encouraged and assisted my partners when help was needed.

_____ I was key to our success.

SATISFACTORY: (S)

_____ My work was complete and correct.

_____ I made several positive contributions to the effort.

_____ I encouraged and assisted my partners at least once.

_____ I helped my group succeed.

UNSATISFACTORY: (U)

_____ I could have done better.

_____ I not help or encourage my teammates.

_____ I did not worry about the project.

_____ I kind of goofed off.

Below, justify the grade you have given yourself.

Figure 6.7

CONCLUSION

While all teachers rely on grades for student evaluation and assessment, national tests will continue to constitute a powerful external force in our school environments. The purpose of this book is to help teachers and schools counterbalance these standardized assessments with ongoing meaningful, authentic assessments of student understanding.

Assessment is the means whereby teachers can judge what their students have learned and where instruction needs to be refined. Assessment also provides teachers a way to gain valid insights into their students' thinking and reasoning abilities. Consequently, assessment becomes a powerful tool to help teachers monitor the effectiveness of their own teaching, judge the utility of the learning tasks, and consider when and where to go next in instruction.

Armed with the strategies and tools included in this book, you, the reader, are now ready to meet this challenge.

Glossary

assessment the process of gathering information about what students know and can do

behaviorism a branch of psychology closely associated with education that espouses the use of reward and punishment to modify behavior

bell-shaped curve (or **bell curve**) a symmetrical curve, usually plotting a continuous frequency distribution (tally of the number of times a particular type of event occurs), such as a normal distribution, which looks like a cross section of a bell

benchmark a standard used for judging a performance; defines the quality level of a student's work

cognition the information a student learns, understands, and knows

content standards statements about what students should know and be able to do; describe the knowledge and skills that students should acquire

curricular objectives goals or objectives outlined in a curriculum, encompassing both content and performance standards

evaluation the process of interpreting and making judgments about assessment information; the process of determining whether students have learned the objectives

Internet the superhighway of cyberspace; refers to the global information system that is logically linked together by a globally unique address space based on the Internet Protocol (IP) and that provides, uses, or makes accessible, either publicly or privately, high-level services layered on the communications and related infrastructure

metacognition thinking about thinking (the ability to self-reflect); a higher-order cognitive skill

neuroscience any aspect of science dealing with nerves, parts of nerves, or the nervous system

open-ended question (also referred to as **free-response question**) any question for which there is more than one correct answer; usually involving an explanation of the solution strategy

performance standards indices of quality that gauge the degree to which content standards have been attained

progress criteria standards by which a student's growth and progress are measured; stated in relative terms as the manner in which a student progresses from novice to basic or proficient

rubrics guides that give direction to the scoring of student products and/or performances, or standard guides

software the programs run on computers (the hardware)

testing one of the tools of assessment; a measuring instrument used to document student learning

References

Balkcom, S. (1992, June). Cooperative learning. *Education Research Consumer Guide,* No. 1, ED346999.

Burger, S. E., & Burger, D. L. (1993). Challenging technical news for performance assessment. *The CRESST Line,* pp. 6–7.

Caine, R. N., & Caine, G. (1994). *Making connections: Teaching and the human brain.* Menlo Park, CA: Addison-Wesley.

Caine, R. N., & Caine, G. (1997a). *Education on the edge of possibility.* Alexandria, VA: Association of Supervision and Curriculum Development.

Caine, R. N., & Caine, G. (1997b). *Unleashing the power of perceptual change: The potential of brain-based teaching.* Alexandria, VA: Association of Supervision and Curriculum Development.

Caine, R. N., Caine, G., McClintic, C., & Klimek, K. (2004). *12 Brain/mind learning principles in action: The fieldbook for making connections, teaching, and the human brain.* Thousand Oaks, CA: Corwin Press.

Gardner, H. (1983). *Frames of mind: The theory of multiple intelligences.* New York: Basic Books.

Gardner, H. (1987). Beyond IQ: Education and human development. *Harvard Educational Review, 57*(2), 187–193.

Goleman, D. (1998). *Working with emotional intelligence.* New York: Bantam Books.

Goleman, D. (2005). *Emotional intelligence: Why it can matter more than IQ.* New York: Bantam Books.

Johnson, D. W., & Johnson, F. (1987). *Joining together: Group theory and group skills* (3rd ed.). Englewood Cliffs, NJ: Prentice Hall.

Johnson, D. W., Johnson, R. T., & Holubec, E. J. (1994). *Cooperative learning in the classroom.* Alexandria VA: Association of Supervision and Curriculum Development.

Kendall, J., & Marzano, R. (1996). *Content knowledge: A compendium of standards and benchmarks for K–12 education.* Aurora, CO: McREL.

Mathis, W. (2003). No Child Left Behind: Costs and benefits. *Phi Delta Kappan, 84*(10), 679–686.

Mauer, M. M., & Davidson, G. (1999). Technology, children, and the power of the heart. *Phi Delta Kappan, 80*(6), 458–460.

McTighe, J., & Ferrara, S. (1996). *Assessing learning in the classroom.* Washington, DC: National Education Association.

National Commission on Excellence in Education. (1983, April). *A nation at risk: The imperative for educational reform.* Washington, DC: U.S. Government Printing Office. Retrieved from http://www.ed.gov/pubs/NatAtRisk/index.html

National Council of Teachers of Mathematics. (2000). *Principles and standards for school mathematics.* Reston, VA: Author.

National Research Council. (1995). *National science education standards.* Washington, DC: National Academy Press.

National Research Council. (2000). *How people learn: Brain, mind experience and school.* Washington, DC: National Academy Press.

No Child Left Behind Act of 2001. Pub. L. No. 107–110, 20 U.S.C. 6311.

Popham, W. J. (2001). *The truth about testing: An educator's call to action.* Alexandria, VA: Association of Supervision and Curriculum Development.

Popham, W. J. (2003, January). The debasement of student proficiency. *Education Week,* p. 8.

Ronis, D. (2001). *Problem-based learning: Integrating inquiry and the Internet.* Arlington Heights, IL: Skylight.

Sylwester, R. (1995). *A celebration of neurons: An educator's guide to the human brain.* Alexandria, VA: Association of Supervision and Curriculum Development.

Tomlinson, C. A., & McTighe, J. (2006). *Integrating differentiated instruction and understanding by design.* Alexandria, VA: Association of Supervision and Curriculum Development.

U.S. Department of Education. (1998, February 27). *FY 1999 annual plan: Vol. 1. Objective performance plans and data quality.* Retrieved from http://www.ed.gov/pubs/AnnualPlan/index.html

Whitehead, A. N. (1979). *Process and reality.* New York: Free Press.

Wiggins, G., & McTighe, J. (2005). *Understanding by design* (2nd ed.). Alexandria, VA: Association of Supervision and Curriculum Development.

Index

CORWIN PRESS

The Corwin Press logo—a raven striding across an open book—represents the union of courage and learning. Corwin Press is committed to improving education for all learners by publishing books and other professional development resources for those serving the field of PreK–12 education. By providing practical, hands-on materials, Corwin Press continues to carry out the promise of its motto: **"Helping Educators Do Their Work Better."**